THE GOSPEL
FOR THE PERSON
WHO HAS EVERYTHING

WILL WILLIMON

PARACLETE PRESS
BREWSTER, MASSACHUSETTS

2020 First Printing This Edition

The Gospel for the Person Who Has Everything

Copyright © 2020 by William H. Willimon

ISBN: 978-1-64060-540-4

Original Edition Copyright © 1978, published by Judson Press

Library of Congress Cataloging-in-Publication Data
Names: Willimon, Will, 1946- author.
Title: The gospel for the person who has everything / Will Willimon ;
    foreword by Lillian Daniel.
Description: Brewster , Massachusetts : Paraclete Press, 2020. | Summary:
    "A guide for those who wish to live a deeper, fuller life of faith in
    Christ"-- Provided by publisher.
Identifiers: LCCN 2020006792 | ISBN 9781640605404 (trade paperback) | ISBN
    9781640605411 (epub) | ISBN 9781640605428 (pdf)
Subjects: LCSH: Christian life--Methodist authors.
Classification: LCC BV4501.3 .W55358 2020 | DDC 248.4/87--dc23
LC record available at https://lccn.loc.gov/2020006792

10 9 8 7 6 5 4 3 2 1

Published by Paraclete Press
Brewster, Massachusetts
www.paracletepress.com

Printed in the United States of America

Contents

Foreword
Lillian Daniel

I first heard about Will Willimon the way I heard about the best punk rock bands, back in the days when I played the bass in one—through bootleg tapes. Three years after breaking up a band called Geek so I could attend Yale Divinity School, I was suddenly ordained and preaching in Cheshire, Connecticut. How had I ended up in the pristine suburbs, playing pastor, in a parsonage next door to the New England church when all my cool friends from grad school were still getting their noses pierced with impunity?

To add insult to injury, my new congregants, many of them educated professionals, expected me to bring, from my own master's degree, my "best practices" in two areas: fundraising and church growth. Unfortunately, I didn't recall covering either subject in school. Their third expectation was so obvious to them that it didn't bear stating, but once again, it had not been anywhere near the top of the list of required subjects in seminary. They also expected me to be an excellent preacher who would connect their lives to Scripture. While we had covered the importance of the preaching task in school, when I look back, what we were really being trained to do was deliver lively lectures, which today I would say is an oxymoron. So in those early days of ministry, in the midst of the growing knowledge of my own incompetence, I began to do what my master's degree had trained me to do—feverish research and skim reading.

It was then that I discovered the voice of Will Willimon, when a clergy friend slipped me a copied tape of sermons that I would later purchase honestly myself for full price, not because I was that good but because they were that good. Up until then, recorded sermons seemed to be the purview of televangelists and celebrity preachers whose ministry challenges concerned broadcasting in Russia rather than, say, keeping the attention of a dwindling confirmation class. Will's call to preach to resident aliens gave me much more purpose than the preacher who was hawking his own purpose driven life.

It was Willimon's voice that did it for me, with an accent like my South Carolina relatives, the intellect of my Connecticut professors, and the courage of a prophet in exile in Babylon. Listening to him take apart a parable was like standing next to a famous chef dicing up an onion, where the smell both makes you hungry and then makes you cry. When I heard his sermon "No Way to Run A Farm" I was two years ordained, but in that moment it was as if I was newly called.

And later, after discovering what a prolific author he was, I was so relieved to discover that he brought no jargon into the writing task. I heard and felt his spoken preaching voice in the words on the page, crisp to the ear, blunt and often hilarious. Long before we had met, he had become for me a role model for authenticity in the church, back in the days before "authenticity" was simply a buzzword for oversharing and self-promotion. His authenticity was that of the respectful polemicist. Not only was he unafraid of an argument, he also made you feel worthy because he was taking the time to argue with you. I wanted to write like that one day.

In 2013, I wrote a book called *When "Spiritual But Not Religious" Is Not Enough: Seeing God in Surprising Places, Even the Church,* which ignited a conversation across Catholic talk radio, PBS, the *Christian Science Monitor, Christianity Today,* and the *New York Times.* The chum I threw into the water attracted all kinds of sharks who either applauded or condemned me for saying this:

> Being privately spiritual but not religious just doesn't interest me. There is nothing challenging about having deep thoughts all by oneself. What is interesting is doing this work in community, where other people might call you on stuff, or heaven forbid, disagree with you. Where life with God gets rich and provocative is when you dig deeply into a tradition that you did not invent all for yourself.

At that time, as today, the church was being divided into categories of "liberal" and "conservative," thus playing out American Christianity's habit of taking the worst practices of the political or business world and doing them badly, decades later. So people who tracked these sorts of things were surprised to see that my book was getting talked about on both "sides," including those who believed my gender barred me from being an actual pastor, but who appreciated the point I made in this imagined encounter in a chapter entitled "Spiritual But Not Religious? Please Stop Boring Me":

> On airplanes, I dread the conversation with the person who finds out I am a minister and wants to use the flight time to explain to me that he is "spiritual but not religious." Such a person will always share this as if it is some kind of daring insight, unique to him, bold in its rebellion against the religious status quo. Next thing you know, he's telling me that he finds God in the sunsets. These people always find God in the sunsets.

My written words elicited howls of complaint from mainline Protestants who were, like me, on the side of women ministers, gay marriage, PBS tote bags, and recycling programs that bordered on works righteousness. In other words, these were "my people," and while they confessed to agreeing with what I had been thinking about, they called me out for the sin of saying it in print, where the unchurched might actually read it. Their logic seemed to follow that of many denominational church leaders who are convinced that unchurched people, in their spare time, thirst for nothing more than to seek out and understand internecine theological squabbles. They scolded me by saying, "Yes, we all feel that way about the SBNR's but you can't tell them that!" But what part of the word "them" would Jesus have used in such a condescending context? And what part of their tacit charm school silence will benefit the many hurting people with a God-shaped hole they have not yet diagnosed for themselves?

Sometimes the good news comes with a confrontation, or at least a little irony.

As a writer and as a preacher, I confess the person next to me was a composite "straw man," and certainly was not a single real person. Let's be honest, on a real airplane, where I might at some point need help with my oxygen mask, I would never berate my seat mate by saying what I did in the interior monologue:

> Thank you for sharing, spiritual-but-not-religious sunset person. You are now comfortably in the norm for self-centered American culture, right smack in the bland majority of people who find ancient religions dull but find themselves uniquely fascinating.

Believe it or not, at the time I wrote that, I had never read nor heard of the book called *The Gospel for the Person Who Has Everything*, by one of my favorite authors. I had never read the trenchant argument that you are about to experience here, that will connect you to people who have seen all this before, from Bonhoeffer's "Man of Strength" to Paul Tillich's "member of the late church," to my own "sunset person," whom Will Willimon described like this:

> Secure, content, competent, reasonably happy and fulfilled, such persons of strength go their own way without any apparent discomfort at having missed the benefits of the Christian faith. . . . What do you say to the person who says, through his or her neglect of the faith, "Thanks, but I don't need it"?

I had never read chapter five of the book you now hold in your hands, which begins much like my own book began, with our author trapped making small talk not in an airplane but at a party punch bowl "in the kind of monologue that tempts a minister to try to conceal his or her profession when at a party." Nor had I read Willimon's next words to the reader, where he says, "What he said to me at the party was not original or profound. It was more annoying than malicious. You have heard his line before, I'm sure."

Decades before, I had written about the "Spiritual But Not Religious" Willimon was wrestling with the same questions I was, and his book, written years ago, now stands up as a classic. Long before we were starting to use "SBNR" to describe a group large enough in number to deserve their own acronym, Bonhoeffer and Tillich and so many others have wondered how to speak to the person who thinks she has no need of God. As I read all this now, I realize that my questions and complaints are nothing new, and that I am no more special or unique as an apologist than the person I was sitting next to on the airplane. Nor is the controversy new, although each generation experiences that a little differently.

In my own case, I recall some pretty personal attacks, often covertly related to gender or age. Since several chapters in the book had appeared first in blog posts, a common response was to imply that I was a thoughtless poster of rants and screeds, rather than a writer who had tested out my material before in multiple venues. "Did you even think before you hit send on that? Perhaps you should have waited until you were less emotional," they said, and one even asked if it was my "time of the month."

Little did they know that every word in my book had been edited in the harshest and best way, by the Holy Spirit in conversation with real people. I think I learned to do that from Will Willimon, whose writing always has a conversational feel, which, as any writer knows, is a form of writing that takes an incredible amount of work. Different from academic discourse, you can feel the passion behind ideas that have actually been debated in coffee shops, dive bars, and yes, even in pulpits, like Duke Chapel, where Will Willimon preached for so many years as Dean of the Chapel, and where he first invited me to preach. That was the first of a number of visits to Duke that allowed me to develop my own writing ideas in guest sermons that I inflicted upon that unique congregation of religious mutts before tucking my tail and returning home to New Haven, or Chicago, or now, to my home in Iowa.

If you know the Duke Chapel, it is more like a cathedral than a chapel. Massive in scale and stature, it draws students and a regular smaller congregation of members and then a ton of tourists from Durham, North Carolina, to Durham, England. Visitors come as they do to other monuments and museums of the faith, to hear the choir, to see the art and architecture, and some even visit to see if God is still speaking, although no one checks for religious intentions at the church door.

Duke Chapel always struck me as the perfect Petri dish in which to try to converse with both the seeking and the ones who don't think they are missing anything. So it was there that I preached a word I had tried out and edited over the years, and that sermon ended up gelling into the controversial chapter. That Sunday, the after-church conversations were the beginning of my hunch that the unchurched tourists had much more in common with the people in the pews on a regular basis: they all liked being challenged; they appreciated irony. But later I would articulate that both groups, my own church board members included, were terrified to talk about faith in a world that would label them as bigoted or obnoxious, and therefore kept silent. It was for these brilliant souls that I wrote *Tired of Apologizing for a Church I Don't Belong To*, which continues a conversation from a sermon I gave at Duke Chapel, in the pulpit Will Willimon filled for so many years, where I first tried out some provocative ideas in a pulpit that he had first invited me to fill as a guest speaker, as a younger preacher and author.

So when people have told me I should have thought more carefully before hitting send, I've always been grateful to be able to say that not only were my words edited and shaped over the years but that they were finally knit together by the Holy Spirit at Duke Chapel, where I got the best critical feedback of my preaching life.

I believe that the fact that I could get that writer's gold of both constructive critique that Sunday at Duke was a result of the culture Will's preaching and writing had created there. It is a culture he creates with his reader in books like this one, honoring us with points of view we may be baffled or even offended by, because he trusts us to be able to withstand a new thought or two. In a world where we are quick to take offense and cut one another off, Will continues to hone the art form of the whimsical yet generous polemic. Agree or disagree, you will not find yourself saying that the observations in this book are not true. In *The Gospel for the Person Who Has Everything* you can tell that he has come by his views honestly, as a pastor who loves God, listens to the people around him, and then shares the stories with the rest of us.

Lillian Daniel *is a preacher, teacher, and writer in Iowa whose most recent book is* Tired of Apologizing for a Church I Don't Belong To.

Preface
To the New Edition

Years after writing his momentous *Romans* the great theologian Karl Barth reread his world-famous book. Much had happened to Barth in the intervening years since he had written *Romans* in his first, forlorn parish. After reading, Barth exclaimed, "Well roared, lion!" I'm not Barth nor is this book *Romans*. Still, I'm happy and honored that my work from long ago is being again set before the church.

Picture a young pastor, a couple of years out of seminary, stuck in a congregation by a bishop who said, "Son, do what you can, and we promise to rescue you in maybe a year or two." Two years passed without the good folks of Trinity United Methodist pledging the budget or fixing the leaking roof. Nevertheless, Duke Divinity School somehow thought it wise to invite inexperienced, unsuccessful me to teach seminarians. The dean welcomed with, "Publish!" So, sitting at our kitchen table, I reworked one of my articles from *Christianity Today* ("Congratulations," said the CT editor, "first timers usually don't get this much negative mail"), strung together five or six of my sermons from Trinity, called it "The Gospel for the Person Who Has Everything," and had my first "church book."

Orson Welles said that a person's best work is done before age thirty-five or after seventy. Though this septuagenarian is not feeling too creative at the moment, the continued life of this little book may prove Welles half right. After four decades, the work of a callow, untested thirty-year-old preacher lives again. I'm pleased to see that, before I met Stanley Hauerwas, served Duke Chapel and the episcopacy, or wrote eighty other books, even in my youth, I wasn't too shoddy a preacher.

My rereading of *The Gospel for the Person Who Has Everything* surprised me: From the first days I was already working some of the themes that characterized four decades of ministry. I've changed and grown along the way but not as much as I thought. Though kept standing in the wings, Karl Barth was behind many of my arguments—and Kierkegaard too. In this book are Barth and Bonhoeffer for everybody: grace and law are two sides of the same work of the same God, God is so much more interesting than we are, and salvation is integrally tied to vocation. Though, I should note that Barth would disapprove of my apologetic intent and Bonhoeffer would challenge some of my interpretation. The book is curiously Wesleyan in its stress on Christ's summons to service, on enacting love on behalf of others in need, and on sanctification as being as significant as justification. Christ calls us not to make our lives a bit less miserable but rather to enable our lives to count as part of his mission in behalf of his beloved in his world. So, here's evangelism the old-fashioned, Wesleyan way rendered into contemporary idiom.

Though there are dated references to Oral Roberts, the Rev. Moon, and Erich Fromm, I'm impressed by the continued relevance of the book's major concerns. That's a bit depressing. The notion that Christ is among us mainly to meet our self-defined needs—that Jesus is a somewhat primitive therapeutic technique for solving our problems and soothing our complaints—is a hard heresy to defeat. In this book I set out to nix the notion that Jesus is here to give you whatever it is you think you must have in addition to Jesus. Judging from many of the sermons I hear, and some that I preach, my goal for this book, to defeat Pelagianism, isn't yet accomplished.

Just this past week I worshiped in a church where the pastor opened the service by plaintively saying, "We are here hurting, anxious, and groaning, seeking answers, lamenting amid the racism, sexism, ageism, and anthropocentrism."

Looking around the gathered all-white, upper middle-class congregation, I thought they seemed in pretty good shape. A congregation of modern, relatively affluent, North American folk like us need pastoral encouragement to be even more self-centered and self-consumed? Can worship be reduced to a weekly deep dive into our innate narcissism?

Decades before we learned to label our theological pathology as moralistic therapeutic deism, this little book, for any of its flaws, named it. Perennial is our attempt to turn Paul's "the gospel of God" (Rom. 1:2–4) into a means of getting what we want out of God. But the gospel is God's means of getting what God wants out of us.

When Methodists stop talking about God, we enjoy talking about ourselves. How is it in your church? Without God, we are free to fall face down into the worst excesses of carping moralism and saccharine sentimentality. Except for a few notable lapses, by the grace of God, I'm glad to see that in this book I avoided both. The book's title begins, not with my attempt to assess human need but with the word "gospel"—the most interesting (and ultimately truthful) word the church has to say to the world of any age.

Sure, there's the awkward phrase, an occasional sappy illustration, a cringe-worthy idiom or two. Although I like the opening sentence that states our pastoral ease "with the person in the gutter rather than the person at the top," I wish I hadn't ended the book with a paragraph that sounds close to a blathering platitude by Joel Osteen. That makes me even more grateful that Lillian Daniel—one of the most clear-eyed, risk-taking, tell-it-like-it-is, platitude-free preachers I know—overlooked my youthful indiscretions and wrote this edition's foreword.

Still, for any of its faults, I'm rather pleased with the book's straightforward, eager-to-be-heard style. I'm surprised that a thirty-one-year-old, novice theology professor, fresh from a little, nowhere Methodist congregation, had the self-confidence to lay aside concerns about what my sophisticated theological friends might think, or how my inexperience and ignorance disqualified me, and just say the good news of God that people deserve to hear. I don't remember feeling self-confident at the time. A 300-member congregation that no one has ever heard of, where the treasurer sheepishly says, "If you can't find a way to make these deadbeats put more in the plate, you won't be paid this month," had not instilled in me self-confidence.

I therefore believe that any strength in the book is attributable, not to the poise or solid academic preparation of a young preacher, but rather to a reckless God who saves by capturing unqualified people like me and using them—even though they be unaware and ill-prepared—for good purpose. Perhaps I talk about risk and vocation so much in the book because three years into ordained ministry, I was still reeling from the shock of God having picked me, of all people, to deliver the word.

That vocative God—Father, Son, and Holy Spirit—is so much more interesting than the rookie preacher who wrote this book. Yet I am bold to believe that the gospel announced by and embodied in that God explains me and this book.

Original
Preface

Protestant theology and preaching have an easier time with the person in the gutter than with the person at the top. We follow Martin Luther who followed Saint Augustine in thinking that the chief sins are human pride and self-assertiveness. An admission of utter helplessness and total wretchedness is usually considered to be the first necessary step on the road to salvation.

Our gospel seems tailored to fit only the downcast, the outcast, the brokenhearted, and the miserable. We think we do an adequate job of comforting the sad and uplifting the depressed. But what do we say to the strong, the mature, the joyous persons in our midst?

In my role as a parish pastor, I frequently meet men and women who, from all which I can observe, are happy and fulfilled human beings. Some of them are rich; some are poor. Some of them are powerful leaders in business or a profession, and some fulfill their callings in more unassuming roles. These people of whom I speak share the common characteristics of maturity and personal strength. They seem to be the kind of integrated, resourceful, balanced people whom most churches I know need so desperately.

And yet, it has been my experience that these are the very people who do not relate well to the church. They seem to find their fulfillment, their challenges, their support elsewhere. What pastor has not coveted people like these for his or her congregation? They could be the dynamic leaders, the inspiring teachers, the supportive, caring persons whom every congregation needs. But who can blame them for, in effect, saying to the church, "Thanks but no thanks. I can get along without it"? Perhaps the message and life of the church have been directed exclusively toward the wretched and the sad to the exclusion of the strong and the joyous.

For a long time I have tried to tell these people that they really can't get along without the church, that they are *really* not as happy and fulfilled as they seem to think they are. But now I am having second thoughts. Perhaps they *are* indeed happy and fulfilled. Perhaps our preaching and theology have left them out altogether. Must one be sad, depressed, wallowing in sin and degradation, immature, and childishly dependent in order truly to hear the Good News? (See chapters 1 and 2.)

I don't think so. I rejoice that the church has had something good to say to the wretched, the dispossessed, the outcast, the weak, and the dependent people throughout the ages. We have had something to say to such people, and sometimes we have, by the grace of God, said it well. Now I want us to ask ourselves, "What do we say to the strong?" (See chapters 3 and 4.)

This book is not for everybody. I am addressing myself here to a particular group of Christians and potential Christians. I want to speak to the strong and to the people who are weak and want to be stronger. I do not say that these persons of strength have no needs; rather, I say that they have peculiar kinds of needs which require a particular kind of evangelistic message. They have their sins, but these sins are not the sins of the weak (chapter 5). We will then talk about worship which takes God's strong love seriously (chapter 6) and ethics which arise out of our response to that love (chapter 7). Finally, we will speak about the church as a place of continual growth and widening responsibility (chapters 8 and 9). While I discuss preaching and sermons in the first chapters, I only use sermons as illustrations of some of my main points. In other words, I am writing for the people who hear sermons as well as for those who preach.

In my last church, we had an adult discussion group which helped me form many of the ideas in this book. That group of lay persons was constantly in my mind as I wrote this book. I have tried to keep the chapters short for group discussion.

Finally, I here acknowledge my debt to my past congregations at Broad Street and Trinity United Methodist Churches in South Carolina and to my students at Duke Divinity School. These people first helped me to see that the glory of the Christian faith is that, rather than devastating us because of our human weaknesses, it delivers us by building on our God-given strengths!

"The LORD is my strength and my song,
  and he has become my salvation;
this is my God, and I will praise him,
  my father's God, and I will exalt him."

Song of Moses
Exodus 15:2

You Have a Problem

I n my part of the country and in my part of the Protestant tradition, "testimonies" are big. A testimony is usually a time when one stands up in front of other people and publicly testifies to what God has done for him or her. It is sort of a spiritual autobiography. In many churches, testimonies are a part of Sunday morning worship. Sometimes testimonies are confined to smaller groups.

I have never given a testimony myself (until I got bold and wrote one at the end of this chapter); but I have heard a number of testimonies, and I have always been interested in other people's testimonies. Telling one another our life stories is usually always illuminating. But what amazes me is that in nearly every testimony I have heard, there has been invariably an unoriginal, typical, predictable pattern. Usually, the pattern goes something like this:

> I was miserable. I was lost and tormented by guilt over the way I had been living. I had tried everything, and nothing seemed to work. Then I found Jesus, asked him to come into my life, and since then my life has been filled with joy.

It is not surprising that such an experience might happen to a person. The New Testament contains a number of stories of tormented people whose lives were transformed by a new relationship with Christ.

What is surprising to me is that this should be the only pattern for *everyone*. One would be hard pressed to find many examples of the "I was miserable—then I found Jesus" type of conversion experience in the Gospels. Look at the many ways people are called by God in the Bible. Abraham, a rich and contented desert sheikh, was out gazing at the stars one night. Moses was a murderer hiding in the wilderness. Isaiah was at prayer in the temple. Peter was fishing. The little man in the tree was curious. Matthew was at the office counting money. Paul was on a pious errand. We are all individuals. We all have different names and faces and different strengths and weaknesses. The Bible shows that we are always called by our very own names in the particular way God chooses to touch us. The Bible seems to say that there is no one way to be called. The "One Way" T-shirts and bumper stickers of the Jesus Movement are a mistake. And yet, 90 percent of the testimonies which I have heard would lead one to believe that God is unable to speak to anyone who has not first reached an appropriate state of misery.

Our "I was miserable—then I found Jesus" testimony pattern is partly the result of the testimonies of some famous people in post-biblical times rather than the result of the way the Bible tells it. Sometimes Paul is used as a prime example of the "I was miserable—then I found Jesus" pattern of salvation. In chapter 3 I'll try to show why Paul's conversion was not that way at all. No, it is to a number of later Christians that we owe our "I was miserable—then I found Jesus" pattern. Augustine's guilt and tormented conscience over the wild oats which he had sown as a youth; the long, introspective struggle of Martin Luther which finally led to his vision of a merciful God; and John Wesley's difficult search in which his self-doubts were finally assuaged when his heart was "strangely warmed" have all become part of our Christian conversion lore. So much are they a part of our lore that these experiences, along with other similar conversions, have become *the* stereotyped way of relating to God.

But the Bible reminds us that this is not the one and only pathway to God. Augustine, Luther, and Wesley probably never intended that their experiences should become a set of rules for attaining salvation. But their testimonies were particularly dramatic, and they gave their testimonies particularly well, and the rest of us who have followed after them haven't been very original in finding our own paths to God.

Testimonies have caused me other problems as well. Personally speaking, my life story never seemed as interesting as most of the people who stood up and told theirs. I have been a sinner, but never a very spectacular sinner, never a very glamorous sinner. My past contains a number of stumblings and actions for which I am not too proud; but I can boast of no juicy, dark episodes during which I wallowed in sin and utter depravity.

Nor was I assailed by serious doubts or agonizing struggles of faith. The existential *angst* which many people go through in late adolescence seemed to elude me. I had my questions, and I was a mild iconoclast at times. But none of this makes for very exciting testimonies. I seem to have had the misfortune of growing up in the church in a mildly Christian environment and to have been at least passably happy most of my life. In short, my own life story just does not fit the "I was miserable—then I found Jesus" pattern.

Theologically speaking, I've got some other problems with the typical testimony motif. First of all (and this may be unfair of me), too often the testimonies I've heard slip into a kind of religious self-righteousness. They have a distinctly "Me graduate school Christian—you kindergarten Christian" sound about them. They are filled with such shopworn clichés as "Since I found Jesus . . ." and "When I decided to give my life to Christ. . . ." From what I know of the Bible, the story there is usually that few of us can boast of finding Jesus; he finds *us*. And the important thing is not what I decide about God but the fact that, in Christ, God has decided for *me*.

Once, when Martin Luther heard a man bragging about how he had "accepted Jesus Christ as his Lord," Luther (in his usual crusty manner) said, "Big deal! What are you patting yourself on the back for? If a rich man walks up to a poor man on the street and hands him a sack with a hundred dollars in it and that poor man then accepts the gift, think how absurd it would be for the poor man to go about bragging, 'Look at me. I was wise and good enough to accept a gift of a hundred dollars.'"

My inevitably halfhearted acceptance of Christ is always overshadowed by God's prior, wholehearted acceptance of me.

Secondly, I am uncomfortable with the subtle selfishness which I hear behind the "I was miserable—then I found Jesus" pattern. I resist the idea that Christianity is a kind of payoff. I don't see how

I can come to God asking for the curing of all my headaches and heartaches, doubts and depressions, sadness and sorrows and then move from this essentially self-centered and self-serving religion to a religion centered upon the praise and service of God. I don't see how one comes to the faith out of selfishness ("God, make *me* unmiserable, make *me* happy, make *me* fulfilled") and ends up with the kind of selflessness which I see in the life and teachings of Jesus. I don't see how one can turn Christianity into a crutch to support one's dependencies and end up standing as a child of God on one's own two feet. It's little wonder that many people seem surprised and a bit baffled when their preachers dare to mention some of the ethical demands of the gospel. Many of them have signed on to the faith with only the expectation of rewards and are thus baffled with all this talk about responsibilities.

My third theological problem with the "I was miserable—then I found Jesus" pattern is related to the main point I am trying to make in this chapter. I am troubled by the notion that Christianity is little more than the last hope of a miserable person who has tried everything else and now, in utter desperation, decides to "try" God. I call this the "there are no atheists in foxholes" syndrome. The hackneyed observation that "there are no atheists in foxholes" out on the battlefield is no credit to God or to ourselves. When we are down and out, when the battle is raging and bombs are bursting in air, when we are frightened half out of our wits, then, of course, we are willing to give anything a try—even God. But is this a particularly noble path to faith? It may be one way to get close to God, but I question whether it is the most desirable way. It makes us too much like that distant cousin who never bothers to write or visit us until he falls on hard times and needs some quick cash. Any of us can testify to the shallowness of our foxhole pledges and conversions. How many times have we all promised, "God, if you will just let me get over this problem, I'll . . ."? When the shelling stops and we're safe, foxhole conversions are notoriously short-lived.

How much greater credit to the power of the Christian gospel it is for a person to be able to testify:

I was happy and fulfilled. Each day was sheer joy to me, and life was a shower of blessings. Then Jesus showed me how much greater joy life could be when I rose above the selfish pursuit of my own happiness and the preoccupation with my own problems. In losing my life for others and for him and his work, in using my blessings for something greater than myself, I found my true life.

But that is precisely what we don't testify, preach, or teach as being the Good News. We seem to offer a faith which has good news only for those who are in search of some kind of external dominance or deliverance. Christianity is presented as that blissful reward which is won only at the end of a long, agonizing, tormented journey through the "dark night of the soul." It is the celestial food which can only be enjoyed by those who have first whetted their appetites through misery and emptiness or through gorging themselves in the fleshpots of sin and depravity.

I have noted that there are many people who do not seem to relate to the "I was miserable—then I found Jesus" scheme of salvation. I call them the "strong ones." They represent the kind of personal strength which does not relate to the "there are no atheists in foxholes" syndrome or "our misery first—salvation afterward" conversion pattern. These are people who seem to be saying to us through their absence in our churches and through their lack of interest in our faith, "If that is all there is to Christianity, then I can get along without it."

They seem to be reasonably happy, fulfilled, and content. Their lives appear to have enough meaning, enough balance, enough sense of self-worth to make life basically enjoyable for them. I do not say that they are "religious," and I do not claim that they are "Christian." I merely say that they seem to be the kind of mature, integrated, strong individuals whom the church needs and for whom the practice of our faith calls. What are we to do with them?

I'll tell you what we usually do with them. We usually try to shrug them off by saying, "You may *think* that you are happy, fulfilled, useful, mature. But you are really miserable. You've got a problem, and your problem is that you are too full of self-deceit and pride to know that you have a problem. And that is your problem." Our actions remind me of the hypochondriac who suffered under so many real and imagined illnesses that, when he finally got well, he became convinced that his health was some new and strange illness!

But who are we kidding? To become strong is not our sickness but our salvation. Down deep I think we know that these strong ones are not too far from the kind of humanity we all would like to have. We are deeply threatened by their apparent lack of wretchedness, their seemingly self-sufficient style, their disgusting sense of self-fulfillment. It would seem from our reaction to them that if a person suffers from neither oppressive guilt nor devastating despair, then there is little which the gospel can say to such a one.

Recently, I was talking with a friend of mine who directs the campus ministry at a nearby college. I asked him what type of student was attracted to his campus ministry center. "Oh, we only attract one type of student. We get the sick ones. We get the ones who are lonely or continually depressed or unpopular or frightened by what they see and hear on campus. We don't get the popular ones or the bright ones. The leaders do their leading elsewhere. The self-confident ones don't seem to need what we have either. We get the ones who can't do any better than come here."

That is a bleak picture not only of our version of Christianity's appeal on a college campus but also of its appeal just about anywhere else. Granted, we have a faith which has a uniquely comforting word to speak to the sad. We have a Lord who proclaims healing for the sick, freedom for the enslaved, hospitality for the outcast. But are those the only people for whom we have a place? Jesus had compassion for the weak. He healed the sick. But he did not ignore persons of strength—rich people like Zacchaeus; big, husky hotheads like Peter; intellectuals like Paul. Luckily, Jesus was too good a physician to offer everyone the same medicine! He told the rich young ruler to give it all away, but he let Zacchaeus use his wealth as his faith demanded. He gave a more detailed exposition of the faith to Nicodemus but tossed a simple "Follow me" at Peter, the big fisherman.

I get the impression that we offer the same medicine to everybody. We don't take the time or trouble to do individual diagnosing. Victor Borge tells the improbable but delightfully absurd story of his old uncle who spent all of his time discovering cures for sicknesses. The only problem was that there weren't any illnesses to match the cures which his uncle invented! Tragedy struck when his uncle gave his aunt some of the medicine for an illness which she didn't have and she died the next day from the cure! Are we in the church trying to offer cures for illnesses which some people do not have?

Perhaps we have no one to blame but ourselves and our simplistic theology if these strong ones assume that the Christian faith is little more than an opiate for those who have need of a dependency, a protected hothouse environment for emotional weaklings, or a simplistic explanation of life for intellectual midgets. Is it right for us to bring forth the gospel, telling everyone, "You have a problem"? Maybe, just maybe, their problem may not be *that* problem.

It is something to think about.

My Testimony

As you now know, I am not particularly fond of most of the testimonies which I have heard. But if I had to give a testimony of my own in order to tell you something about myself and where I am coming from, then—at the risk of committing all of the sins I have mentioned earlier—I suppose that the testimony of my own journey of faith would go something like this.

I was born into a reasonably happy home. I was baptized in my grandmother's living room by a Methodist country preacher who used a prized silver bowl of my grandmother's.

I don't remember much talk about religion during my childhood. But I do remember being in church nearly every

Sunday, sitting there being scratched to death by my wool trousers and choked to death by my starched collar as the minister prayed those interminable prayers. I also recall Bible stories read before breakfast nearly every morning. I remember long, fun summers playing in the fields and woods around my house, homemade ice cream, trips to the homes of admiring relatives, and mostly good days at school. I remember arguments among my uncles about politics and the president, and I remember the death of my grandmother. I remember not being able to play baseball very well and feeling left out because I couldn't play. But, basically, I remember a kind of boyhood world in which the universe seemed to be a fairly dependable, basically friendly sort of place where there was much to learn, many places to visit, inhabited by many interesting people.

I can't remember a time when it was not assumed that I was somehow a part of God's great, good scheme of things. Once I asked my grandmother if I was a Christian or not. "Of course you are," was her reply. Her reply seemed adequate and natural for me, as natural as if I had asked her if I was a boy or if I was going to college when I got older. It was a faith which one not so much decided for or struggled with; one just got it and grew into it the same way I got my southern accent and my first Sunday suit.

I did do some rebelling of sorts. I can remember having many questions in high school about the Bible and the faith. I can remember wondering if the scientific explanations of things which I had learned in school somehow nullified what the Bible had to say about things. I can remember some of the nasty feuds which went on periodically in our hometown church and wondering if the church was just as full of problems and as sinful and petty as any other organization in our town. I can remember the cruelty of racial segregation and the disillusionment of seeing some very fine people do some very cruel things to other people simply because of the color of their skin and simply because "it had always been done that way." Those experiences taught me some things about original sin.

I avoided the church for a while; I even wondered if the Christian faith wasn't for me at all. I had gotten the impression that the best way to be a Christian was to turn off your brain, close your eyes to reality, and shut yourself in a closet of self-centeredness. The "blind faith" which I was urged to cultivate seemed more like a sickness than an attribute. I didn't have "blind faith," and I didn't want it.

A number of experiences helped lead me back to the faith where I had really always been. A couple of tough college courses in religion which were taught by good professors convinced me that the Christian faith is not weakened by rigorous questions and examination; it is strengthened by such activity. I realized that the mystery of the divine in our midst is a deep, swiftly running stream which is not dammed up or circumscribed by our always too puny religious notions. I discovered that there was enough in our faith to keep me on my tiptoes peeking for a better vision, craning my neck for a closer look, as long as I lived. Some people say they lost their religion in a college religion class. I found mine there.

It was also during my college years that the Civil Rights movement was at its peak. There were people in clerical collars at the head of those marches. There were some usually mild-mannered Southern preachers, whom I knew, who were sticking their necks out and risking themselves with their congregations to preach some courageous sermons in behalf of racial justice. I knew some of them, black and white, who suffered for their courage; and their suffering and their boldness convinced me that Christianity does not have to be a sedative for soothing pained consciences or a justification for our cherished prejudices.

In short, I was caught off guard by the faith. I was surprised to hear within the words of the Christian faith about as tough a challenge, as high a calling, as strong a voice as I ever hope to hear.

2

Bringing Them to Their Knees

f I could sum up about 90 percent of the sermons which I hear (and a lot of the ones which I have preached), the summary would go something like this:

1. You have a problem.
2. Christ is the answer.
3. Repent and be saved.

It makes little difference whether the sermon is being delivered by a conservative, biblical fundamentalist or a liberal, social activist. The pattern is usually the same, even if the content and the slogans are different.

The traditional style of preaching begins by noting assorted evidences of the wretched state of humanity. "All have sinned and fallen short," it will tell us. "We are full of pride, self-righteousness, false self-security, and idolatry. We have built a materialistic, sensualistic, heathen society." The preacher may then throw in a few juicy examples of our utter depravity. Recent divorce statistics may be cited, or it may be the statistics on drug abuse, suicide, teenage pregnancies, etc. Then the sermon goes on, "We are unworthy of God's love. We are guilty as charged. Our foolish pride (said to be our chief sin) has led us to try to live life on our terms and not on God's terms; therefore, we are miserable."

"You really stepped on our toes today, preacher," many people will say as the preacher shakes their hands at the church door after the sermon. This comment may indicate either (1) that we view religion essentially as an exercise in clerical sadism ("giving them what they deserve") mixed with its counterpart of congregational masochism ("thanks, I needed that") or (2) that what we really

meant to say was, "You really stepped on *their* toes today, preacher."
The perversity of this style of preaching is illustrated in the fact
that many preachers consider it a great compliment to be told
that they have "stepped on people's toes." This is an interesting
criterion for a good sermon, one which we will need to examine
later.

Only after the bad news are we given the Good News (gospel).
The gospel comes in the form of an answer, a solution to our
problem. You know how much we love answers and solutions.
Unlike people of old who used to be fascinated and a little bit in
awe of mystery (e.g., Moses kicking off his shoes before the burning
bush), in our scientific, technological world, we see mystery as a
problem to be solved, a question to be answered, a program of
action to be followed. In our elementary science class, we learned
the "scientific method" of approaching problems: the problem
must be clearly stated; then alternative solutions must be found and
experimented with. When the best solution is found, our problem
is solved. Any soap commercial which begins with the words "An
amazing scientific discovery . . ." or "Scientific tests show . . ." is sure
to sell soap.

This history of Christian preaching shows that this scientific
approach to problems has greatly influenced the way sermons
present the gospel. Most of our sermons begin with an analysis of
the human condition. That condition is conceived of as a problem,
and a wretched problem at that. (Somehow, when traditional
Christianity looks at humanity, it always manages to see us at our
worst.) But if humanity is the problem, then what is the solution? If
our destiny is the question, then what is the answer?

Christ is the answer! All the other answers and solutions which
the world gives to our problems and our questions are insufficient.
We are told: "Put your faith in Christ"; "Accept Jesus Christ as your
personal Savior"; "Take Jesus into your heart"; "Give your life to
Christ." Most of these phrases have become so shopworn and vague
that the majority of the people has no idea what any of them really
mean, and the church usually does a poor job of helping people
see what "giving one's life to Christ" might actually look like in

their daily lives. But if "a soft answer turneth away wrath," we seem to feel that a vague answer—"Christ is the answer"—turns away tough questions.

If Christ is the answer, then how are we to apply this answer to our question? We are only interested in theoretical science so far as it can become applied science. We're not as interested in gaining knowledge for the sake of knowledge as we are interested in gaining knowledge which we can use. If Christ is the answer, what are we supposed to do? Here we come to the third and final point in our traditional sermon outline: Repent and be saved.

Note that repentance precedes salvation. Repentance can mean a multitude of things. To most of us, it means to feel sorry that we are who we are and that we've done what we've done. Repentance is thus conceived of as a feeling that we have been naughty. The trouble with this definition of repentance is that feelings are notoriously slippery and short-lived. Modern sensitivity group leaders and old-time tent revivalists may tell you that feelings are all that religion is about. Just get a proper feeling inside, and you are certified as religious.

Classical Christian theology, at its best, has maintained that repentance is more than just a feeling, more than just an emotional sense of unworthiness. Repentance is an action—not just a once-and-for-all action, but a continuing action. Repentance involves a turning away from something and a turning toward something else. In the Greek language of the New Testament, repentance is *metanoia*. *Metanoia* literally means "a change of mind." It is not a feeling but a chosen attitude based upon God's love. When a young man and woman stand before a minister in a marriage ceremony, the minister does not ask, "Do you feel like you love each other?" The minister asks, "*Will* you love each other?" Feelings are fine, as far as they go; but the church demands that we base a marriage on something more than just feelings. The adulterous woman came to Jesus, repented, and was forgiven. Then Jesus said, "Go, sin no more." *That's* when the repentance began and continued—in a change in life and a change in action, more than just in a change of heart.

And it is precisely here, I think, that most preaching and most theology break down. Too much of them are simple exercises in clerical scolding and guilt building. Repentance, defined as a feeling of unworthiness and utter wretchedness, becomes the goal of not only the sermon but life in general as well. This is true not only of the more traditional pulpit-pounding, hellfire-and-brimstone preachers of a generation ago (including those holdovers of this style who crowd the airwaves on Sunday mornings) but also of the avant-garde liberals with their "prophetic" social messages. The older ones used to go after the smoking, drinking, and cursing sins. The newer ones go after racism, capitalism, and conservatism. Both assume that merely by condemning people and convincing them of their mistakes, they can force people to do better. But merely pointing to people's sins and getting them to feel sorry for those sins will not eradicate their sins. This is what Reinhold Niebuhr used to call the "fallacy of all moralistic preaching." Paul laid bare the weakness of this homiletical style when he observed of his own life, "the good that I would like to do, I cannot do" (see Romans 7:19). People can't always do what they want to do, no matter how bad the preacher makes them feel about it. They are usually more the victims than the villains. They are trapped. *And part of their entrapment is their cowering sense of unworthiness and impotency which we foster with our moralizing and condemnation.*

Repentance of the "feeling sorry" variety does not lead to salvation. The word "salvation" comes from the same word from which we get our word "salve," the ointment which one puts on wounds to help them heal. Salvation means to be healed, to be made whole. Moralistic scolding and guilt building seem only to pour salt on people's wounds or open new wounds. Nobody gets healed or saved from or for anything. People are converted into pious doormats who are incapable of the kind of health and wholeness which a life lived with Christlike boldness would demand. The traditional "repent and feel sorry" approach to the Christian life leads to the sense of personal frustration, negativism, and despair which is in the hearts of too many struggling Christians who have been bombarded since birth by this clerical scolding and berating.

Why does this "You've got a problem—repent and be saved" style continue to be popular? I had to ask myself that question a few years ago when I was serving in my first church in a little corner of rural Georgia. I gave out questionnaires to all the members in the church, asking them on which subjects they would like to hear more sermons. The members responded almost unanimously that they would like more sermons on "hell and damnation." These people were poor, deprived, and had very few opportunities or advantages. They had been victimized by a host of ignorant, if well-meaning, lay pastors. They had been misled into thinking that religion is an exercise in self-degradation and self-depreciation.

I pointed out to them that there is a difference between the preaching of John the Baptist and the preaching of Jesus. John came preaching in the traditional mode, "Repent or be swallowed up in the fire of hell!" Jesus had a different message. Jesus preached, "Repent because the kingdom of God is here!" Do you see the difference between the two sermons?

John preached a message of warning, full of threats of dire consequences and punishments for sin. He wore a rough coat of camel's hair (a symbol of repentance and mourning). He said of the One coming after him, "His shovel is in his hand to winnow the grain. The wheat will go into his barns, and the chaff will be burned in an everlasting fire" (see Matthew 3:12). One gets the distinct impression from John's preaching that he assumed that he was dealing with more chaff than wheat!

Of course, John the Baptist came to "prepare the way." He was not the way but only the precursor of the way. Some people say that children usually feel that their parents are threatening them before they learn true obedience. They say children first must fear their parents before they learn about parental love. Perhaps the preaching of John represents a kind of immature, first step on the road of faith. Perhaps. In the next chapter we will consider the difference between immature religion and mature faith.

But for now, let us note that Jesus preached a different message than John the Baptist. John called people to repent in order to avoid the punishment to come. He issued a solemn warning.

But Jesus told people to repent because of something wonderful which has happened before their very eyes. Jesus issued a joyous proclamation. John dealt in guilt. Jesus dealt in grace.

Could this be what Jesus had in mind in that beautiful passage in Matthew 9:35–38?

> And Jesus went about all the cities and villages, teaching in their synagogues and preaching the gospel of the kingdom, and healing every disease and every infirmity. When he saw the crowds, he had compassion for them, because they were harassed and helpless, like sheep without a shepherd. Then he said to his disciples, "The harvest is plentiful, but the laborers are few; pray therefore the Lord of the harvest to send out laborers into his harvest."

Jesus seemed to be saying here that ministers who harass these "sheep without a shepherd" are a dime a dozen. Ministers who see their task as preaching Good News and healing are few.

Scolding and sermonic guilt building are probably due more to the weaknesses and hang-ups of the preacher than to their relation to the Good News. In our contemporary society, most ministers lack the great influence and control over people which they once may have had. Perhaps they compensate for this by flexing their clerical muscle in their sermons. As Colin Morris has noted:

> Let a preacher exhort his people to join him in the struggle for social justice, look back, and find himself marching alone; then it demands almost superhuman forbearance to avoid using the pulpit to purvey Good Chidings rather than Good Tidings. The sermon becomes a twenty-minute tirade which the congregation endures with a stoicism born of long practice, except, of course, for the minority who get perverse enjoyment out of the conviction that the preacher's sharper verbal shafts are aimed at the man or woman in the next pew.[1]

Another reason that preachers try to preach the Good News of Christ in the old style of John the Baptist is that people like it. As I found in that little church in Georgia, something within us gets a kind of perverted satisfaction in having our "toes stepped on." Such preaching does have a ring of truth about it since we all know about our sins and failings better than anyone else could know. The truth hurts, and when we get hurt in a sermon, we know that we stand in the presence of some sort of uncomfortable truth.

But why do we seem to enjoy getting hurt, getting wounded by words, getting scolded and made to feel bad about ourselves and our lives? Perhaps we enjoy getting our toes stepped on because we think that that must be what religion is all about. Religion for us is like bad-tasting medicine. As with mouthwash, we figure that the worse it tastes, the more good it must be doing us. Since most of us see "repentance" as simply feeling bad about ourselves, then the worse we feel about ourselves, the more religious we must be. The more we can show how "humble" we are, the more religious we are. That way, we don't really have to change or do anything. All we have to do is feel. After we have shed a tear, felt sorry about ourselves and for ourselves, then we have done enough. It gives us a kind of emotional catharsis. That's why feelings and emotions can be enemies of true religion. We get confused into thinking that feelings are all there is to religion. Feelings become a substitute for the conversion—the changing and the turning around— which is at the heart of true repentance. "You really stepped on our toes today, preacher," we say after the sermon. With the preacher standing there on our toes, it's easier for us. No one could expect us to move or get up and go anywhere with a parson in a black robe standing on our toes!

As any child will confirm, sometimes a spanking is not the worst punishment. If your mother spanks you for stealing cookies from the cookie jar, then you can focus your angry feelings on mother and the spanking. The punishment helps you forget about how you have deceived and disappointed your mother, and that forgetting makes it easier for you. If she should spank you very hard, then you will feel that you have earned the right to steal a few more cookies simply to console your hurt feelings. Sometimes the most effective "punishment" is for a parent to go on loving and doing for a child in spite of the many times that child falls short of the parent's expectations. Most good parents raise their children this way and usually prove more effective in the long run as disciplinarians than the spankers. Likewise, a verbal beating from the pulpit can often shield us against our own inner awareness of how we have deceived and disappointed ourselves and God. If the preacher scolds us for our racism and prejudice, we can get mad at the preacher for daring to "meddle" in controversial issues. Or we can join with him in devastating ourselves for our sin. Either way, a real change in life or habits (conversion) can usually be avoided. Hellfire-and-brimstone sermons delivered by either tent revivalists or social activists can thus have their advantages!

The fallacy of such moralistic scolding and berating, the weakness of the "You've got a problem—repent and be saved" scheme of salvation, the reason why so few people really change under the influence of such a message is that it gets the Good News backward. Karl Barth once said, as we have been saying here, that too much Christian preaching speaks about an obligation which must be met in order to receive a gift, whereas the real message of the New Testament is about a gift which then leads us to an obligation. In our traditional sermon outline, repentance attempts to come before grace, whereas grace always precedes true repentance.

Why? Because before you truly feel the unconditional, unending, unqualified love of God, you are virtually incapable of complete honesty about yourself. It takes a secure, stable, confident person to admit that he or she can be wrong. When a parent stands over a wee toddler, looks down on him, and asks, "Johnny, did you steal cookies from the cookie jar?" an intelligent toddler will either lie about it or run and hide under the bed. Threatening parents do not produce a climate which fosters honesty. In the same way, the repentance that comes from a fear of God's wrath or an attempt to "apple-polish" our way into God's approval is usually shallow repentance. It is mere "playacting," as Karl Barth once said. We repent just enough to get back into God's favor. We admit to just enough sin to convince God we are not totally ignorant of our shortcomings.

We can't afford to be completely honest or completely open because we're not completely sure that God's love is permanent. Therefore, we must try to keep some shred of our own self-respect, some seemingly credible excuse for our actions. "I'm not all *that* bad," we say. "Sin is only when you murder or steal. Sin is not my little falsehoods and white lies." Thus, we cannot afford to lay all our cards on the table for fear that God controls the game and that the game is totally against us. Our "repentance" becomes another part of our elaborate defense system of false images and rationalizations through which we attempt to protect ourselves and our self-respect from the attacks of a God who is not our friend.

Humanly speaking, that's why Christians advocate the long-term commitment of marriage over the relatively insecure arrangement of a man and a woman just "living together." "Living together" outside of marriage is fine if all you want out of love is a superficial feeling and a few short-lived good times. But if you want a chance to be totally honest, open, and encountered by another human being, if you desire one permanent human relationship amidst the transitoriness and shallowness of most of our relationships, one relationship where you are free to take off your mask and stop playing games, then nothing provides that like the commitment to a covenant with another person "for richer, for poorer, in sickness and in health," which marriage gives us. As long as there is the easy possibility of one person in the relationship walking out the door forever, no real honesty is possible. The grace of knowing that as a couple you are "in this together forever" gives you the freedom to admit to your problems (confession) and thus to start being healed (salvation).

The old style of preaching begins where it ought to end. It begins by dwelling on human problems and shortcomings (sin) by telling us, "You've got a problem." Then it puts forth Christ as a panacea for all our problems. Or it tries to bring us to our knees by threatening and abusing us: "Repent and be saved." If it can get us on our knees, sufficiently remorseful and devastated, then it dangles out before us the payoff, the solution: "Christ is the answer." We must "accept Jesus Christ and be saved."

As I stated in our discussion of testimonies in the last chapter, the manner in which traditional theology and preaching approach the faith ends up distorting the faith. We come to faith either out of fear, out of utter devastation, or out of an attempt to make a deal. Our lowest human natures are appealed to in an attempt to raise us to the highest ideals of Christ. It doesn't work. The result is disciples of Christ who have come to him out of a fear of God as an enemy or out of a devastated and therefore dependent personality or out of an attempt merely to use God to get the things they want.

It seems to me that the Bible says that true conversion (turning, change, rebirth) comes at the point when a person realizes that the God who was once considered to be a powerful enemy, who was to be avoided or bargained with is, in reality, a friend who is to be trusted. Just when we expect to get clobbered for our guilt, we get clobbered by grace. We realize that, in our frantic search for peace and happiness, we have looked in the wrong places and have overlooked the God who has always been looking for us. God does not have to destroy us in order to deliver us. We do not have to give or say or pay anything. In Christ it has all been given, said, and paid for us. We do not have to make any kind of deal with God. In Christ love has been dealt our way. And it is a permanent love which does not walk out and slam the door on us when we have been naughty, which does not threaten us, which does not desert us when we are poor and sick and ugly. It is a love which loved us before creation and loves us now with only one thing in mind: to love us through eternity.

This love, this grace must always come first. The trouble with moralistic preaching is that we get too concerned over what we are supposed to be doing for God and forget what God has done, will do, and is doing for us. The trouble with the "You've got a problem—repent and be saved" scheme of salvation is that it begins with us—our problems, our needs, our feelings, our beliefs—and forgets about God. Repentance is not simply a matter of feeling sorry for our sins. Our sincerity and our humility are not what make our sins forgiven. Our sinfulness is forgiven as a gift from God. To be told, "*If* you will feel sorry, and *if* you are sincere, God will forgive you," is to take forgiveness out of God's hands and put it in our hands. Contriving feelings of "humility" and "wretchedness" in order to get forgiven can be just as manipulative of God as our thinking that our sins are forgiven by repeating fifty "Our Fathers." Nor is conversion simply a matter of getting down to the altar. We are so preoccupied with the need to "make a decision for Christ" that we forget that, in Christ, God has once and for all made a decision for us! In getting down on our knees to "accept Christ," we overlook the fact that if the life and death of Jesus Christ means anything, they mean that God accepts us! You and I can do little to add to or to improve upon God's acceptance of us in Christ except to say yes to it and enjoy it. To quote Karl Barth again, "'Yes' is all the Christian life is about."

That sounds simple, doesn't it? That sounds easy. Perhaps it sounds too easy. It is, but then it isn't. That grace, that gift (for remember, the word "grace" simply means "gift" in the Bible) from God can be very threatening to us. That gift can be very difficult for us. Why? Because in our "you get what you deserve" and "God helps those who help themselves" world, accepting a gift can be one of the hardest things we are ever asked to do. Humanity has always been infected with the fantasy that we are "self-made men," that we can work for and earn anything our hearts desire. The grace of God tells us that there is nothing about God's love which we can earn, deserve, or work for. It has to be given. It can come only as a gift.

Have you ever noticed how people blush when someone pays them a compliment? They blush because a compliment is an unexpected gift which cannot be repaid. It can only be graciously received or else shrugged off. ("Oh, you don't really mean that," we say.) It may be more blessed to give than to receive. But it is usually more difficult to receive than to give. Especially when the gift can't be repaid. That's what bothers us about the grace (gift) of God's love.

It is threatening to admit finally that we are at the mercy of love. It is devastating to admit finally that we are saved by *grace*. It bothers us to know that first and finally (in the words of Frederick Buechner) there is *nothing* you have to do, nothing *you* have to do, nothing you have to *do* to be in God's good graces. You don't have to feel a certain feeling of either joy or wretchedness. You don't have to believe this set of beliefs or follow that set of rules. All you do is respond the way you respond whenever anyone gives you a gift. All you do is say, "Thanks," and accept it. As Paul Tillich says, "Accept your acceptance." Again, as Barth says, "'Yes' is all the Christian life is about."

Martin Luther tried to tell us. Augustine tried to tell us. Paul tried to tell us. They all tried to tell us that we are "saved by grace." But we think it all sounds too simple, too good to be true. Martin Luther protested against the "works righteousness" of the rites and duties which people were using in the medieval church to try to earn God's grace and forgiveness. Luther discovered that grace is a gift. But we heirs of Luther have reverted to another kind of "works righteousness" of our own by making correct beliefs or correct actions or correct feelings prerequisites for salvation. Despite Jesus' warning to us against attempts to "save ourselves," we would rather do it our way than God's way. The church condemned this heresy (Pelagianism) a long time ago, but we still practice it just the same.

The church has always tried to make this point clear in the rite of baptism. Whether it be the infant baptism of Lutherans, Roman Catholics, United Methodists, Episcopalians, etc., or the adult believer's baptism of Baptists, Adventists, and Jehovah's Witnesses, both modes of baptism are intended to illustrate the power and givenness of God's grace. Baptism is ultimately not something we do but something God does. It is at God's initiation that we are baptized and brought into the family of God. Baptism is thus a kind of adoption ceremony, a public sign that we are heirs of God's gift in Christ. The churches which practice infant baptism demonstrate that God comes to us before we come to him. God claims us as his children before we claim him as our Father. God believes in us before we believe in him. What is more helpless, more dependent than a little baby? For that matter, what is more sinful (jealous, selfish, self-centered, frightened) than a little baby? And, therefore, what is more representative than a baby of the way we always live with God, not only as infants but as adults! The churches which practice adult believer's baptism say essentially the same thing about unmerited grace, but in a different way. Their baptism of adults says that the church is not something that we build but something that God calls together. God's grace calls forth our faith. There are no second-generation Christians. God calls forth each generation fresh in its own time, giving the gift of his grace with each new generation, calling on each new generation to say yes to God's divine Yes as that generation has heard it in Christ.

That's why the traditional pattern of preaching and theology must be reversed. It is a child of our "works righteousness," "everyone for one's self, you get what you deserve" culture. It begins with us ("You've got a problem"); then it attempts to get us to our knees ("Repent . . .") so that salvation (". . . and be saved") is the payoff, the reward for our righteous achievements. It turns God's love into a bit of candy which is given only after we have first swallowed the bad-tasting medicine of repentance. Show me a child who spends his life trying to earn his parents' love, and I'll show you a child who has a lot to learn about the nature of parental love. There is nothing a child can do to make his parents love him more. Their love comes as a gift. The traditional sermon assumes that we have it within ourselves to save ourselves, change ourselves, heal ourselves. It tells us that we must be brought down to our knees before we will be allowed to stand on our own two feet before God. It tells us the things we must do *if* God is to love us, whereas Jesus told us about a God whose love contains no "ifs" at all.

3

Standing On Our Own Two Feet

Having decided that the traditional sermon model and the traditional way of presenting the Good News are really bad news, let us now shift the sermon model we began with in the last chapter so that it now looks something like this:

1. Christ is the answer.
2. You have a problem.
3. Repent and be saved.

Now we begin with Christ, with the love with which we have been loved. We begin with what God has done, not what we may or may not do. We begin by reflecting upon God's "Yes" to us before we think about whether we are to say no or yes to God. For us, Christ becomes the answer that stands, not at the end of all our selfish desires and fearful questions, but the answer that stands before we even knew or dared to ask the most important of life's questions. He is the answer which makes our question, "What must I do to be saved?" irrelevant and unnecessary. Rather than debate what we need to do to get saved, we rejoice in what God has done in Christ to save us. We switch from the threats of John the Baptist to the proclamation of Jesus. Grace comes first.

Grace comes first because that is what we need to be reminded of first. Beneath all of our striving and working and frantic efforts to achieve God's good graces is our cowering inner sense of unworthiness. Our chief sin is not the sin of pride. Our pride is merely our way of dealing with our sense of unworthiness. Dana Prom Smith writes in *The Debonaire Disciple*:

When a father tells his son to "go out and make something of yourself," the father is implying that the son is not worth much at the time. Guilt, a sense of unworthiness, and a feeling of inadequacy undergird a system of virtue that is rooted in achievement.[1]

The reason that we are so threatened by John's preaching, the reason that we rush about trying to believe the acceptable belief or feel the acceptable feeling or do the acceptable deed is that, in our insecurity, we try to prove ourselves in order to counter the accusation that we are not up to God's standards.

The temptation to try and earn our way into God's favor is especially appealing to people of white middle-class backgrounds. Most of us, from the time we were children, have been told by our Depression Era parents that we must work for what we want and that we can get what we want in life only by dedication, education, and persistence. As Wayne Oates noted in his *Confessions of a Workaholic*, many of us get confused into thinking that hard work is the answer to *all* our problems and needs. We get trapped on a perpetual treadmill of getting and earning and achieving until the day when, having worked ourselves to death, we discover too late that the most important things in life cannot be earned or achieved. They come as undeserved gifts.

Many persons of strength who have been successful in earning the material things of life assume that work must be the way to achieve the spiritual things as well. But the message of Christ is good news about a status which we already have with God, which we don't need to "earn" and can't work for. You can't work to earn the right to be your father and mother's child. You already are that child. The realization that you are a child of God, that this is a gift and not an achievement, is the point where conversion starts.

Then and only then can we start to talk about our real problems. Then we are able to talk about our needs as God's children and heirs, not about our needs as human beings in general. Our problem is not, "What can we do to get God to love us?" Our problem is, "What can we do in light of God's love for us?" As Thomas Aquinas used to argue, only when we sense the permanence of God's love for us can we see how fickle our love is toward God. Only when we sense the truth in God can we sense the falsehood in ourselves. Karl Barth once said that only Christians are sinners. Only Christians? Barth meant by this that only people who know how much they are loved can ever sense how much they have betrayed that love. Only people who have heard God's "Yes" toward them can see how puny and wavering has been their "yes" toward God. When Paul lamented the fact that "the good that I would do, I can't do," he was talking about his life after his conversion to Christianity. Unless we first sense that "Christ is the answer" and has always been our answer, then we will continue to occupy ourselves with minor problems which are not our real problems. We will continue to worry about what to believe, how to feel, what to say, how to act. Until we first sense the grace of God in Christ, we will be unable to see that our real problem lies in our anxious posturing, self-depreciation, and self-justification with which we are trying to earn what we already have as a gift. God has made us all somebodies, but most of us live our lives as if we were nobodies.

True repentance comes now. We don't have to play games or wear masks or make excuses. We can now admit who we are because we know that God will not destroy us because of our admission. As we said before, it takes strong, secure persons to admit that they can be wrong and then to try to right their wrongs. Weak, insecure people are forever trying to defend themselves, make excuses for themselves, and justify their actions. They do this because they have to. They are rightly hanging on to any shred of self-respect which they have. But the Christian realizes that such defensiveness is unnecessary. We can start to be honest with ourselves in order to change ourselves. In this way repentance does relate to our "salvation" and our starting on the road to the health and wholeness which God has always intended for us. Repentance itself is a gift of grace.

Note the kind of repenting which went on in the episode with Jesus and the woman who was living in adultery (John 4:1–42). The woman comes to the well to draw water and is surprised that Jesus talks to her since she is not only a woman but also a Samaritan. Jesus crosses these traditional barriers to affirm the woman and accept her. He engages her in conversation, and, before the conversation ends, he makes her aware that he knows of her sin and that she is forgiven. Likewise, in reference to the woman who wept at Jesus' feet (Luke 7:36–47), Paul Tillich said, "Jesus does not forgive the woman, but He declares that she is forgiven. Her state of mind, her ecstasy of love, show that something has happened to her. The woman comes to Jesus because she was forgiven,"[2] not because she felt miserable and thought that if she got down on her knees, she would be forgiven. The woman does repent, and she does seem to be changed (converted). But this only occurs because she has first felt the love and affirmation of Jesus.

Remember the story Jesus told about the prodigal son (Luke 15:11–24)? The boy leaves his father's house to "do it his way." He journeys into the "far country" and, for a while, has a great time. But then things go sour for him. His money and friends dry up. One night he is guzzling down cool ones at a swinging singles' bar, and the next night he is eating husks with swine in the pigsty. He has made himself into what the Jews despised most of all—a pig. Then, Jesus said, "He came to himself." The boy says, "Wait a minute. I don't have to live like a pig and eat this slop. I have a father, and I have a home. I am his son. I can return to him and live like a man." I call that "coming to himself" the boy's "conversion."

Note that the prodigal son's conversion did not begin his sonship. He was his father's boy all along, although he had not been living like it. His turning toward home begins when he remembers his father's love for him. Then and there he decides to go back home. As he nears home, the boy prepares a little speech in his mind. He decides that he will throw himself down at his father's feet, that he will admit that he has been a fool, that he does not deserve to be called his son, and that he will be happy just to be one of his father's servants. But when the boy nears home, his father runs and meets him and hugs him. The father doesn't even let the boy get out the first word of his repentant speech. Note that the father is far more interested in finally having his son back home than he is concerned with getting his son down on his knees in confession. The boy expects to be treated like a pauper, but his father puts a ring on his finger and receives him like a prince.

I remind you of this story of the prodigal son in order to illustrate how our Good News should sound. The story follows the sermon outline we have proposed. An awareness of grace precedes repentance and change. First comes the boy's remembrance that his father is "the answer" simply because he is his father and he loves his son. Then the boy senses his problem: the fact that he is living more like a homeless pig than a son of his father. Finally, the boy "repents"; he turns toward home. He returns to find that his father's love is deeper and more gracious than he ever imagined. I'll wager that he was a changed lad after that. One does not experience such grace and acceptance and come away unchanged. He was whole. Rather than wallow in the mire with the pigs, the boy had started to stand on his own two feet as a man, as a son. He was saved. Jesus said that all of heaven goes wild when such a wayward child finally returns home. But let us never forget that we return because we have a home and a father in the first place.

Finally, I appeal to the life of Paul in defense of the revised sermon model. Paul says in the first chapter of his autobiographical letter to the Galatians that he was a good person. For all we know, he was a rather happy person. Nowhere does Paul say that he was tormented or miserable, that he was wretched or unfulfilled. Paul contends that he was flawless in following the law and touching all the bases. He says that he advanced in his religion "beyond many of [his] own age." Martin Luther's later picture of Paul as a tormented, introspective, guilt-filled man is not supported by what Paul says about his life before his conversion to Christianity. That picture looks more like Luther's inner life than Paul's. For Paul, wretchedness was not a prerequisite for salvation and healing.

Then, on the Damascus Road, "he who had set me apart before I was born . . . called me through his grace." In that experience on the Damascus Road and its aftermath, Paul saw that he had been acting more like a homeless child than a son of God. His eyes were opened to the fact that his "religion" was a smoke screen to conceal his pride and self-righteousness which were themselves cover-ups for his own self-doubts. His Pharisaic fanaticism which had led him on a one-man campaign to stamp out the Christian heretics was really the action of a doubting person trying to convince himself of the rightness of his beliefs. Paul thought that he had been serving God when he had really been attempting to appease God. He had not been living as a free man. He had been living as a "slave" to his own inner fears of unworthiness. He had not been obeying the rules out of love for God and his fellow human beings. He had been using his good works to work his way into heaven.

Somewhere out on the Damascus Road, Paul remembered something which he had forgotten. He found something which he had lost. He found, or should I say he was found by, grace. It was there that Paul reclaimed his lost birthright. He discovered how much he had been loved by God in Christ. The Lord said to Paul, "Rise, *stand upon your feet*" (see Acts 26:16a).

Paul says it so well in the eighth chapter of his letter to the Romans, a chapter which should be read at all baptisms and funerals as the most important thing to be said and heard at the beginning and at the end of our lives, reminding us of what we all so easily forget:

> There is therefore now no condemnation for those who are in Christ Jesus. For all who are led by the Spirit of God are sons of God. For you did not receive the spirit of slavery to fall back into fear, but you have received the spirit of sonship. When we cry, "Abba! Father!" it is the Spirit himself bearing witness with our spirit that we are children of God, and if children, then heirs, heirs of God and fellow heirs with Christ, provided we suffer with him in order that we may also be glorified with him.
>
> . . . If God is for us, who is against us? Who shall bring any charge against God's elect? . . . Who shall separate us

from the love of Christ? Shall tribulation, or distress, or persecution, or famine, or nakedness, or peril, or sword? No, in all these things we are more than conquerors through him who loved us. (8:1, 14–17, 31, 33, 35, 37)

The great Danish Christian philosopher Søren Kierkegaard somewhere says that if there is one thing which unites us all, it is our forgetting, our overlooking how much we have been loved. For most of us, our biggest problem is not what we have done or not done, not what we have felt or not felt or believed or not believed, but simply that we have not remembered with how great a love we have been loved. I suppose the basic difference between Christians and ordinary persons is simply that Christians know that they are loved. They meditate on that fact each day. It fills their hours and determines their conduct. It gives them fortitude in times of pain and meaning in times of joy. Our great sin is that we forget, betray, or treat so carelessly that love. As Paul puts it, "Jesus . . . was not Yes and No; but in him it is always Yes. For all the promises of God find their Yes in him" (2 Corinthians 1:19–20a).

A Parable

I am indebted to a young Lutheran pastor who told the following parable on the occasion of the confirmation of a teenage boy into the church. I think it expresses in a beautiful way how the love of God, rather than attempting to get us down on our knees as repentant sinners, strengthens us in such a way that we are able to stand on our own two feet as children of God.

O nce there was a little lion who lived in the jungle. He was born into a noble family of lions, the kings of beasts. But when this little lion was still a baby, something happened one night which caused him to get separated from his parents and from his family. I don't know what caused the separation—maybe it was an earthquake or a blinding storm. At any rate, the little lion woke up the next morning to find himself all alone in the world. He began to wander through the jungle looking for a family and a home.

Finally, after walking a very long time, he came upon a flock of sheep which were grazing in the meadow. He came out of the jungle and watched them as they ate the green grass.

"This must be my family," the little lion said to himself. "I'll go over and join them."

The little lion went over and joined the sheep. But the sheep paid him little attention. He was so small that he just blended in with them. The little lion watched the sheep as they ate grass and tried to copy them. He wanted to be just one of the flock. He didn't like his first few mouthfuls of grass. And his neck started to hurt from bending over to eat. But by working at it, after a few days he got the hang of it and could eat grass as well as any other sheep. He also worked on saying, "Baa," like the other sheep. But his "Baa" never sounded just right. By day he would wander out across the meadow with the sheep, and at night he would huddle close together with the rest of the flock. It bothered him that his fur didn't seem to grow as long and woolly as the other sheep's. But they were all too busy eating grass and following the leader to notice him; and so the little lion just kept eating grass and following the leader of the flock, too. In fact, he was starting to feel right at home.

Then one day something happened which changed all that. While the flock was out grazing in the meadow, a loud, thundering, earthshaking roar came out of the jungle. All the sheep immediately stopped eating and huddled together in fear. Then there stepped out of the jungle a gigantic, noble lion. He gave out another earthshaking roar. The leader of the sheep started running as fast as his little legs could carry him, and all the other sheep followed after him.

But something told the little lion not to run with the sheep. Something fascinated him about the majestic-looking figure which was emerging from the jungle. He was frightened by him but also drawn toward him. Then, the big lion let out another roar and spoke to the little lion.

"What in the world do you think you're doing?" the lion asked. "Who, me?" responded the little lion.

"Yes, you. What are you doing wandering around with those sheep? And eating grass? And saying 'Baa'? You look ridiculous, and you sound ridiculous."

"But I am supposed to eat grass and say 'Baa,'" said the little lion. "All the sheep do it."

"You are not a sheep!" roared the big lion, roaring so loud that all of the jungle shook.

"Not a sheep?" asked the little lion in complete puzzlement. "No! Just look at yourself. Come over here and look at yourself in this pool of water."

The little lion timidly edged over to a pool of water where the big lion was now standing. He stood at its edge and gazed into the water. To his utter amazement he saw there, not a white, woolly sheep, but a small lion. Not as big and strong as the big lion, but, nevertheless, it was a lion.

"See," said the big lion, "those teeth, those eyes, that fur, those claws don't look like a sheep's. You are one of us. You are a lion."

He was right. The little lion could see that he was right. The little lion realized that all this time he had been trying to be something that he was not, something that he didn't even really want to be.

From that moment on, the little lion became a real lion. He learned to roar and hunt and tame the jungle with the best of the lions. He learned to stand on his own feet, not simply to follow the leader of the flock. He discovered who he was and who he was meant to be.

Somewhere in here there's a lesson for each of us.

"See what love the Father has given us, that we should be called children of God; and so we are" (1 John 3:1).

4
Christianity—Not for Babies

I take as my text something Paul said in his letter to the church at Corinth. The Corinthians had their problems—problems with speakers-in-tongues, self-righteousness, gluttony, sex, ignorance, etc. In short, Corinth was a church about like any other church which has ever existed. Paul says to them, "When I was a child, I spoke like a child, I thought like a child, I reasoned like a child; when I became a man, I gave up childish ways" (1 Corinthians 13:11). This statement comes in the middle of Paul's famous "Hymn to Love," one of the most sublime parts of the New Testament. He tells the Corinthians that they are suffering from a deficiency of Christian love. And here he describes what makes Christian love special.

I have a high regard for this passage, but I have always been puzzled over why Paul says, "When I was a child . . . when I became a man, I gave up childish ways." What does acting like a child have to do with love or the lack of love? Could Paul be saying that in order to love as a Christian loves, you have to be grown up? Do you have to become an adult and give up childishness? I have come to the conclusion that this is exactly what Paul is saying.

Whatever Jesus meant about "becoming little children," he did not mean for us to become childish. We have all heard sermons on this saying of Jesus which extolled the virtues of "childlike" faith and the "innocence and simplicity" of little children. Most of the sermons which I have heard which urge us to "become like children" are an insult to children and adults. "Childlike faith" is often a nice way of saying that a person is emotionally unstable, dangerously naive about life, and has an inherent tendency not to think. Jesus, who gave us such a strong and muscular example of a courageous life lived in the midst of the real world and its evils, does not fit the picture of "childlike faith." There was nothing childish about his life.

But growing up is not easy for us. From the time we were pulled, kicking and screaming, out of our mother's womb to the time we cut the apron strings and walked out the door for our first day of school to the night of our high school graduation when we suddenly realized that we were on our own, we know how painful it can be to grow up. Maturity requires us to cut the apron strings and venture out a hundred times in life. That venturing out is risky and frightening.

Maturity does not necessarily relate to our age. We have all known teenagers who are far more mature than their parents. And we have seen people in their fifties act like infants. Maturity involves becoming responsible for our actions, caring about someone else besides ourselves, and facing up to reality. We don't need a psychiatrist to tell us that, within all of us—at whatever age we are—there lurks a little, thumb-sucking, frightened, dependent child, just waiting to pull us back into childishness. It is never easy to do what Paul urges, to grow up and give up childish ways.

And what bothers me is that the church, far from helping people grow up, too often babies people and perpetuates their childishness.

For instance, the pastor is often depicted as the parent who presides over a conglomeration of children. It is no accident that in the Roman Catholic tradition the minister is called "Father." In many congregations the pastor becomes the father/mother figure for the church. The pastor becomes the advice giver, confessor, arbitrator, disciplinarian, and benevolent autocrat of the Communion table. And most people love it. Dr. Robert Schuller, of *The Hour of Power* TV fame, urges ministers to become the unashamed dictators of their congregations. Schuller guarantees that this clerical paternalism will produce larger congregations. There are probably enough grown-up children who are looking, not for Christ, but for mommies and daddies, to make Schuller's approach successful. It can be reassuring to think that there is someone in a black robe and clerical collar who can tell us what to do, what to think, and how to act. It may be reassuring.

Whether it is realistic or Christian is another matter. I was once told by a professor in seminary that I would have to wait until my hair turned fatherly gray before I could hope to be an effective minister. My hair seems to be falling out before it turns gray! Oh, well, there are bald-headed fathers, too.

Earlier, we examined the dominance-deliverance style of much preaching today. This style of preaching fits in well with the parent-child atmosphere which pervades many congregations. The preacher ascends into the pulpit to scold the naughty children, reveal their shortcomings, and accentuate their problems. He has a right to berate and scold since he is chief disciplinarian and parental figure for the congregation. In spite of what they say, most children like authority figures and enjoy being dependent on someone to tell them what to do. In nearly every group of children, there is always one who is only too happy to be an authority figure and boss everyone else around. Every gang of kids has its leader or bully and a herd of mindless followers. Too many ministers become willing victims of this parent-child syndrome. The implication of such parent-child preaching is that if we will only submit and allow ourselves to be dominated by Daddy's religion, Daddy will see that we get delivered from our distress. And Father knows best.

The father/mother style of ministry is not all bad. We all need fathers and mothers. In times of personal crisis and turmoil, the wise, firm hand of a fatherly or motherly pastor on our shoulders may be just what we need to comfort and fortify us. In our modern world with its absentee fathers and mothers, where children are often denied their right to parental influence and example, a minister who serves as a surrogate parent figure may be needed by many people.

But the Christian faith is concerned with helping people to find their own self-worth as children not only of earthly parents but also of God. Faith has to do with independence, daring to stand on our own two feet, and boldness and risk in behalf of others. If we are forever dependent on some father or mother figure to do our believing for us, will we ever find faith for ourselves? The best pastor is one who leads people to God, not to himself or herself. The best minister is one who leads people down the path of faith without trying to make the journey for them.

A preacher friend of mine said that he once had a dream that his church was like a great, dark womb. Inside that womb were many people sitting, waiting to be born, yet not wanting to be born. He dreamed that his job as a pastor was to push the people out of the womb, to be a midwife, to help give birth to people—in other words, to help them to be born and thus to grow up. That's not a bad definition of what it means to be a minister and to be a church. Could this be close to what Jesus meant when he said to us, "You must be *born* again"?

We have said that true faith has certain mature qualities about it. Christian faith, like Christian love, has a maturity; a balance; a responsible, reasonable, bold, unselfish quality about itself. But Christian maturity can be as difficult and painful to attain as physical or emotional maturity. Therefore, the Christian faith is plagued by a host of childish substitutes for full, mature, adult faith. At the risk of being unfair to some undoubtedly sincere expressions of faith (I remind you that sincerity alone does not make something true), let me give a few examples of what I mean by immature substitutes for true faith.

1. The first immature expression of faith which has a large following is called, for lack of a better word, "Fundamentalism." Fundamentalism is a style of Christianity which claims rigid adherence to the "fundamentals" of the Christian faith. This is fine, but, of course, there is disagreement among most of us as to just what the fundamentals of the Christian faith are. Most fundamentalists seem to have no doubts as to what beliefs are absolutely necessary if one is to call oneself a Christian: biblical literalism, the biblical miracles, the resurrection of Jesus, the virgin birth, etc. In fact, most fundamentalists I have met don't seem to have a doubt about anything. In fact, for a fundamentalist, doubt is a downright sin. Many fundamentalists see themselves as preservers of the pure, basic essentials of Christianity against the erosion of belief which has occurred in modern times. If you are not sure exactly what to believe, they will be only too glad to tell you. God needs defenders, they say, and they rush to God's defense against modernistic detractors.

Why should I call such strong faith and firm belief "immature"? Firstly, most fundamentalists, and most children I have known, have an excessive need to be right and to tell nearly everyone else that he or she is wrong. A child, lacking the powers of intellectual discrimination and having a low tolerance for the ambiguities of life, desperately tries to separate all the world into black and white, right and wrong. Most children are threatened by the thought that there can be any gray area between black and white, any relativity in absolute right and absolute wrong. Part of the painfulness of growing up is finding out that life and life's decisions are not that easy.

Secondly, the so-called firm belief and unwavering faith of the Christian fundamentalist may not be as rock hard as it appears on the surface. Psychologists tell us that the fanatical, total commitment of the True Believer is often a kind of cover-up for troubling inner questions and insecurities. Children have an excessive need to be right because they feel that they are so often wrong. The fanatical believer who is always out proselyting others for his cause, attempting to shout everyone else down and convert everyone else to his belief, may, in reality, be desperately trying to convince himself. For such people, Christianity becomes a set of rules, a set of beliefs which must be adhered to. The doubters must be cast out. No questions must be raised. The Bible becomes a sacred rule book and something to be quoted in order to beat everyone else down with it. The Christian life becomes a badge of exclusiveness which separates the insiders from the outsiders.

But how interested was Jesus in checking out people to make sure they had the "right" beliefs? Where do we find Jesus himself espousing the lists of beliefs which the fundamentalists claim are so essential? Using the Bible as an authority figure and a rule book for life is notoriously risky and downright unfair to the Bible. As Shakespeare said, "The devil can cite Scripture for his purpose."[1] The Bible is a living testimony of faith, marked by peaks and valleys, inconsistencies, different points of view, and different expressions of faith. It can be a compass pointing us in the right direction, but it is not a detailed road map telling us every step to take and every move to make. As Abraham found out when he left his secure home and ventured out into an unknown land, there is always a little risk and insecurity involved in following the living God. Fundamentalism tries to remove the risk of faith by reducing Christianity to a set of simple rules and beliefs (such as the so-called "Four Spiritual Laws" of Campus Crusade). But true faith involves trust, and sometimes it means trust in spite of the fact that some of our questions are still unanswered and some of our doubts are unresolved. It is a childish wish of ours to try to remove that uncertainty and risk from the faith.

2. Another expression of immature religion is the attempt to identify a contemporary messiah. The book of Revelation tells us that there are false saviors and true saviors. Everyone who looks like a messiah may not be a messiah. Time and again history has shown us that youth and children are often the first victims of charlatans and demigods. I think of the terrible Children's Crusade in the Middle Ages or the Hitler Youth Movement in our time. Perhaps children are receptive to such false leadership because they lack the balance and perspective that age sometimes gives people. Usually all of us have a few painful experiences of being disappointed by people in whom we have put too much trust before we come to the realization that people are people and that even the best of people have weaknesses and shortcomings. Extremism is an inherent danger to the young. When we are young, we get a piece of the truth, and we think we have all the truth. There is nothing more ignorant than the self-proclaimed wisdom of a college freshman. The less we know, the easier it is to convince ourselves that we know everything.

In our time we have seen a host of self-proclaimed deliverers and their childlike followers. A notable example of this modern messianism is the Reverend Sun Myung Moon's Unification Church. Moon offers a blend of Korean Confucianism, Puritanism, and virulent anti-Communism in post-Christian garb. Moon sees himself as God's chosen prophet to do the job which Jesus failed to do, namely, to establish God's kingdom in the world. Moon's own kingdom of multimillion-dollar industries, influence with an oppressive Korean government, and religious empire are impressive in themselves.

The source of Moon's appeal for his thousands of followers ("Moonies," as they are sometimes called) is not difficult to find. He offers the post-Watergate, post-Vietnam generation a close community life, a rigid moral discipline, and an opportunity for religious commitment and sacrifice which is lacking in most contemporary expressions of Christianity. Moon chides the United States' churches for "becoming senior citizens' homes" and alienating the young. We admit that his criticism has some validity. But the alternative religion which Moon offers is a childish, unbalanced religion. At the heart of Moon's recruitment of new converts is an elaborate system of brainwashing during which the proselyte becomes convinced that Moon is God's only hope for saving the world. "I am your brain. I must do your thinking," Moon unashamedly tells his followers. His followers are not uneducated. Eighty-five percent of the "Moonies" in the U.S. are said to be college graduates.

In a world of dismaying complexity with few simple solutions and few easy answers, where we all stand under the shadow of the threat of nuclear annihilation, Moon's mindless fanaticism has an undeniable appeal. The superficiality of most of our religiousness pales in comparison to the single-minded determination of Moon's followers. While most of the parents of young people who have left home to become "Moonies" rightly speak of the tragedy of having "lost" their children to this modern messiah, there are some parents of new "Moonies" who praise Moon for cleaning up their children, getting them off drugs and onto religion, and giving them "something to believe in again." But is this the function of true religion? The move from being "hooked on drugs" to "hooked on Moon" is not much progress. Too many of his youthful followers have exchanged one form of addiction for another.

I remember reading the story of a young woman who spent two years in the Moon movement as a devoted follower. Her former minister, urged by the girl's distraught parents to try to win her away from Moon's influence, followed her to one of Moon's communes and there attempted to persuade her to come home. She said that the minister quoted to her some Scripture passages and one of the verses stuck in her mind: "The truth will make you free" (John 8:32b). The truth shall make you *free*.

I think that realization helped her do much growing in that moment. She realized that her newfound religion was enslavement to a man—his personality, his beliefs, his ideals, his ego, and his ambitions. She had been forced to give up her family, friends, mind, and personality. The religion which Jesus taught was a way of life which frees us rather than enslaves us. In Christ, we are free to love ourselves so that we may be free to love others. We are free to use our minds and our God-given talents and unique personalities. We are free to become all that we can be. Childish faiths tell us that we must be something else besides ourselves if we are to be saved. Childish faiths smother our individuality, our questions, and our uniqueness in order to dominate us. In our confusing world, the childlike dominance offered by childish substitutes for true faith like that offered by the Reverend Moon may be attractive. But the comfort they offer is not lasting. To be freed by the Truth is to be free indeed.

3. A final example of an immature expression of the Christian faith, the utilitarian approach, is the message of the Reverend Oral Roberts. Dr. Roberts appears to have done some growing and maturing of his own over the years. Those who remember Roberts's image of a few years ago—the tent revivalist and flamboyant healer who made such extravagant claims for himself—note that he looks different now. His style has changed. He is now a member of a mainline denomination, leader of a multimillion-dollar evangelistic organization, and president of a rapidly growing university which bears his name. But in a way, even though there has been a modification of his earlier style, with less emphasis on physical healing and more on healing of psychological ailments (depression, frustration, loneliness) and financial problems, Roberts still offers a message of miraculous cures for the things which ail us.

Roberts's simplistic theology which he outlines in his "Seed Faith" concept gives people three principles for "Abundant Living": (1) God is your source; (2) give, that it may be given to you; (3) expect a miracle. His book *Miracle of Seed Faith* has sold well over a million copies. A key step to "Abundant Living" is the "Blessing Pact," whereby one pledges to give money (preferably to Roberts's ministries) with the expectation of monetary as well as spiritual blessings. "If you want God to supply your financial needs, then give SEED-MONEY for HIM to reproduce and multiply," Roberts says in his introduction to the "Blessing Pact."[2]

"Being a Christian is the best deal a man ever had," says Roberts, who claims that we should "stress the law of return more than we stress our debt to God." He differentiates the Seed-Faith concept from the traditional idea of Christian tithing: "In tithing, you give after you have made the income. In Seed giving, you give *before*, in expectation of return." One must sow a "seed" of expectation in order to receive a miracle. In his book *Miracles of Christ*, Roberts tells us that God gives miracles only to those who expect miracles, and miracles can be cures for everything from our small bank balances to our toothaches. There is never the slightest hint that firm expectation of miracles may not bring about the desired miraculous payoff. Failure or even a negative response from God does not seem to be possible for Roberts *if* one carefully adheres to the Seed Faith technique. "It always works," he says.[3] This reminds me of the scene from the children's play *Peter Pan* where Peter Pan tells all the children that if they just all close their eyes and believe in fairies very, very hard, then the fairy Tinker Bell will appear and do some wonderful things for them.

Once again, like many other immature substitutes for faith, Roberts's simple, utilitarian, businesslike approach to religion does have its appeal. But is it a specifically Christian appeal? Is this the way to pray? Is prayer simply a technique through which we twist God's arm in attempting to get God to give us what we want? Where in the Bible are we led to believe that every prayer is answered just the way we want it answered? Where are we told that we will get all which we want in life without the risk of suffering or pain or sacrifice? I think here of the scene of Jesus in Gethsemane where Jesus prayed in great earnestness and got no for an answer! In Roberts's hands, Christianity becomes a pragmatic method of obtaining gifts and payoffs for self-centered and self-seeking followers of Christ who follow Christ because of what he can do for them. Miracles become, not strange, unexpected divine interventions into the pain of the world, but expected, bargained-for rewards for saying the right words and believing the right way. Roberts has turned miracles into magic.

Oral Roberts has succeeded, in part, because he plays upon our childish fantasies which tell us that we can follow God without the risk of suffering or failure; he plays upon our childish weakness which drives us to follow any handsome deliverer who promises us a quick, three-easy-steps journey out of our wilderness into a promised land of personal bliss. As adults, we should know better.

I do not say that these three examples of immature faith are specifically wrong. Each of them surely contains a kernel of truth in itself. I just say that they are immature and offer us less than the fullness of Christian life and hope which Jesus preached. They offer us baby food when what most of us desperately need is meat. Paul speaks in one of his letters about "spiritual babes" in the church who must first be fed on baby food before they are able to take adult nourishment. He did not condemn these new Christians as being wrong or misguided or evil. Paul just noted that they are as yet babes in the faith. They need to grow. Paul does not scorn them, but gives thanks for these babes in the faith.

But note that he rejoices over his spiritual *adults*, adults who are capable of digesting the real meat of the faith, of gnawing on the very toughest questions which we must face in life without choking on them.

Paul wished that kind of maturity for every Christian. And so do I.

After Paul spoke about thinking and acting and reasoning like a child, he then turned to the characteristics of mature Christian love (kind, generous, patient, long-suffering, etc.). Having spoken of the nature of immature, childish faith and its substitutes for adult faith, let us now speak of mature faithfulness. I will just suggest what I think are a few characteristics of mature faith; perhaps you can think of others.

1. First, mature faith involves *freedom.* Part of growing up is the exciting and frightening growth of your personal freedom. As a child, you are tied to your parents. They make decisions for you, protect you, guide you, limit you. As you become an adult, you assume more freedom for your own destiny. The same should be true of our growing relationship with God. The followers of John the Baptist were troubled by the fact that the followers of Jesus fraternized with sinners and wine guzzlers, and did a lot of partying. John's followers were still tied to a religion of rules and regulations. Jesus spoke of a religion which frees us to eat with sinners in order to save sinners, free to cross racial and political barriers, free to enjoy life, free to die.

Paul spoke about his old faith as "enslavement" and "bondage." He thought that religion was submitting to the harness of the law. On the Damascus Road Paul learned that "for freedom Christ has set us free." He was free from fear, free from his old compulsiveness, free to stand on his own two feet and to live boldly. The old religion of rules and regulations traps us in a never-ending treadmill of trying to do and say that right thing in order to please or appease God. And you know how impossible it is to do and say the right thing always. Christianity says that God loves us and takes us even when we don't do and say the right thing. And so we are free. Having sensed that freedom, we find that the task of doing and saying the right thing becomes easier, for now we live in joy, not in fear; we do and say things for the right reasons, responding out of love rather than out of defensiveness.

Freedom is not always the easiest thing to possess. Within each of us there is the fear of freedom. Moses had to prod the Israelites out of Egyptian slavery and into freedom. It is sometimes easier to dwell in the security of slavery than to venture forth into the unknown territory of freedom. The religion of rules appears to be an easier religion because it tells us exactly what to do and how to act and what to think. You know the feeling that you had as you left home for your first day of school. You were excited about the new venture of school, but you were also fearful of leaving the comfortable, predictable security of home. Life is always like that. But all other things being equal, surely God can use a grown-up child more easily than he can use a babyish child. In my mother's eyes I will always be her child. Thirty years ago I was her little child. I was totally dependent on her for everything. Now I am her big child, and I am free to do more things for her than I could do as her little child. If God had wanted an army of mindless, submissive robots, he would surely have created us that way. But part of God's glory and greatness is that he created us as free beings, capable of obedience and service which is freely given. "The truth shall make you free." Religion which enslaves is childish religion.

2. If one element of our Christian faith is freedom, then another is the willingness to *risk*. Children seek safety and security because their lives are inherently unsafe and insecure. Part of the job of being a good parent is to encourage and help one's children take risks, not foolish risks for the sake of a dare, but the risks which are necessary for growth and fullness of life. The Christian faith is not well suited for safe harbors and island fortresses. It has a way of stagnating when the water gets too calm and placid. Jesus is always "going on before us," beckoning us, like God beckoned Abraham, into new and unknown territory. The religion of the Pharisees was a sure thing with little risk. They knew exactly what was expected of them and exactly what they needed to do to be "good" people. But Jesus slapped their dead religion, calling them as cold as tombs. The Pharisees were so bound to the comfortable security of their old-time religion that they were blind to the miracle of the Savior coming into their midst. As Christians, we are free to risk, ask questions, doubt, try bold things because we are secure in the love which does not let us go, the love of a God who is always in front of us, leading us on. Part of maturity is learning to live without firm assurances, without all of our questions answered, without everything nailed down. That's why faith is best defined not as firm belief but as trust.

3. Children are inherently selfish. They think of themselves and their needs first. This is a necessary part of the human urge for survival. It is good that a baby cries when he or she is hungry and doesn't stop crying until his or her hunger has been satisfied. But as that baby grows, he or she must be taught to give and share and live in community with others. Only a strong, secure individual is free to be *gracious and giving*. Only when we are secure in our own selfhood are we free to be concerned about other people. The first step toward faith may be the rather self-centered and childish question, "What's in it for me?" That may be the first step, but it must not be the last step. Mature faith involves that long journey from "I" to "you," from selfishness to selflessness.

4. I remember, when I was a child, the summer that I drank root beer for the first time. It was the best thing I had ever tasted. I liked my first glass so much that the next night I took all the money I had and bought a gallon of root beer and sat down and drank the whole thing! In the words of the commercial, "I thought I was gonna die!" You see, I was a fanatic and extremist about root beer. Like children, we get a piece of the truth, and we think we have all the truth there is to have.

Part of growing up is the increased *ability to look at all sides of the truth*, to weigh alternatives, to consider all the possibilities.

Children lack the balance and perspective which sometimes come with age. They fail to see that truth is a multifaceted jewel, so enamored are they with the brilliance of one facet of the jewel. Heresy in the church is simply a part of the truth which has been blown all out of proportion. The churches which focus on the end of the world and the last judgment (apocalypticism) every Sunday stress one aspect of the faith at the expense of other aspects. They forget about the teachings of Jesus which remind us not to get hung up on speculations about the future to the neglect of our responsibilities as Christians in the present. Our doctrine of the Trinity, which stresses the likeness of God to a Father, a Spirit, and a Man, is an attempt by the church to hold these diverse aspects of the same God in a kind of unity. Most of our problems as churches and as people come when we lose our balance and fall over into one aspect of the truth at the expense of the rest of the truth.

5. When Paul was writing to the church at Ephesus, he told the Ephesians, "We are no longer to be children, tossed by the waves and whirled about by every fresh gust of teaching, dupes of crafty rogues and their deceitful schemes. No, let us speak the truth in love; so shall we fully grow up into Christ" (4:14–15, NEB). Paul is here noting the impulsiveness of childish faith as compared to the *depth* of mature faith.

In our modern age, too many of us flit like bees from flower to flower, sipping sweet nectar here and there, never alighting anywhere for long. Psychologists who have studied the backgrounds of new converts to current Christian and non-Christian cults have noted, in many of these people, a long pattern of switching from one religion to another many times over a short period of years. The search for a valid faith is probably a good thing. But the impulsiveness and shallowness of their commitments can be a kind of personality sickness. Like the Greek god Proteus, we shift and contort our forms to fit a succession of different religions and philosophies until we can't remember who we were to start with and what we were looking for in the first place. There is a depth, a putting down deep roots, which should come with maturity.

6. Finally, I think there is a certain *objectivity* which comes with maturity. Children are noted for their uncritical acceptance of all sorts of exaggerated and conflicting claims. I can remember the disillusionment and learning which occurred in me when I excitedly sent off for that "amazing, thrilling, miraculous" toy which was advertised on the back of the cereal box only to receive a cheap, worthless piece of junk in the mail a few weeks later. These are the painful experiences which help us grow up. As we grow, we learn to step back from things, to size things up, judge the truth of things. And yet, it's surprising how many intelligent people fall for some rather preposterous sales pitches which are made in the area of religion.

I saw a sign recently in the post office warning people about the deceit of some mail-order shysters: "IF IT SOUNDS TOO GOOD TO BE TRUE, MAYBE IT IS." I think we should remember that warning when it comes to the claims of various religions. One reason that Christianity is a great religion is that, unlike many of the world's religions, it does not promise us no pain and all bliss and joy in life. It focuses upon a Savior who knew that life is sometimes painful, that people are sometimes cruel and disappointing, that things don't always work out the way we think they should work out. That Savior showed us how life can be lived with nobility and gratitude even when things don't work out. Our God did not stand aloof from human suffering and mouth nice-sounding platitudes from the heavens. Our God entered into the world, lived as we must live, and thus overcame the world. There is the source of hope which is based on the facts of life and not on our fantasies.

Childish faith and uncritical acceptance are so dangerous because they set people up for some terrible defeats. I knew a woman who was told by a well-meaning, if misguided, friend that if she earnestly prayed for her cancer to be cured and if she had absolute faith that God would cure her cancer, she would be cured. That woman died a lonely and disillusioning death. She died convinced that either she must not be a very good person or that God must not be a very caring God since her prayers were not answered. I wager that God was as deeply saddened by that woman's suffering and pain as anyone, that God wanted to give her strength to endure her suffering and death, that God also looked forward to the day of final victory over evil and sickness when such tragic events as the sickness of this woman would not happen. The woman, by searching for a false hope which could not be given, missed the real comfort God could give.

Naive, uncritical faith inevitably becomes the first casualty to the vicissitudes of life. From time to time parents in my church have said, "We need to be teaching our children what to believe so that when they go to college, their professors won't be destroying their faith." From what I have seen, college professors in freshman religion classes don't destroy faith. Life destroys unsure faith. If people can get faith by being told by a preacher that something is true, they can just as easily lose faith by being told by someone else that what they believe is not true. In the words of Jesus, we "must be wise as serpents" because there are a lot of snakes in the world, and a childlike faith often crumbles when it is face to face with the hard facts which are part of our experience in an adult world.

And so, brothers and sisters, let us mature in our faith. We have all spoken and thought and acted like children many times and will probably do so until the day when our maturing is completed as only God can complete it. But let us press forward to become adults and give up childish ways. Grown-up Christians with baby minds and "childlike" faith are stunted Christians.

I once knew an older woman whose middle-aged daughter lived with her. The mother was very domineering and possessive of her daughter. She did all the driving for her daughter because she did not think her daughter had the stamina to drive a car on her own. She never allowed her daughter to marry or get a job. She made all of her daughter's decisions. She treated her daughter as if she were a little girl even though her daughter was in her late forties. I suppose that the mother thought she was being a good mother, protecting her child, shielding her child from risk and failure. But in reality she was being a terrible mother. She was loving her daughter in the wrong way. Whereas most love tries to possess the other person and keep that one close, the love of parents for their children must be different. It must be the kind of love which loves so that the child is free to grow away from the parent. It is love which loves in order to give away the beloved child into the freedom and independence of adulthood. If parents don't love like that, they fail as parents. God loves us like that. God loves us in order to free us from all which would enslave us. God loves us in order to let us be free to be all that we can be.

God loves all his children, but he wants them to be grown-up children. As grown-up, mature children of God, we will be, I'm sure, more useful to God and God's kingdom than by being childish grown-ups. So, Paul says, Christian love is not for babies! To be disciples of Christ, we need to be tough and mature, to stand on our own two feet, to have all our wits about us, to be unselfish and unspoiled. Let us all give up our childish ways so that we might be this kind of disciple!

For the Person Who Has 5 Everything

Well, so you're a minister," he said as he sipped his lime punch. "That's nice."

"Yes," I responded. Having the uncomfortable feeling that I was about to be trapped in a conversation which I wouldn't enjoy, I frantically looked about the crowded room for someone to rescue me. "I never cared much for the church," he continued. "Oh, I went as a child. I suppose everyone goes in their childhood. But then I went away to college, got into business for myself, and I just never felt the need of it again. Not that I'm against religion or anything. I consider myself to be quite religious in my own way. I just don't need it."

It was the kind of monologue which tempts a minister to try to conceal his or her profession when at a party. I have always sympathized with doctors who get trapped in corners at parties by someone who monopolizes their evening with talk of enlarged appendixes and stomach maladies. Every occupation has its hazards. My party conversationalist continued, "I suppose that I'm about as good as the next person. I try to live right, support needy causes around town, and keep my little garden in order. I'm happy. And, after all, isn't that what religion is all about?" He emptied the last drop from his punch cup.

"Some people think that's all it's about," I rather halfheartedly replied.

"Well, anyway, I think it's just great you're a minister and all. I'm sure you do good for some people. Lord knows the world needs people like you to help it along."

That was the last I heard. Glancing at my watch, I tried to extricate myself graciously from the conversation, mumbling something about having to go. He slapped me on the back as I edged toward the door. "Great talking to you, preacher. Maybe we'll get together over at the church sometime."

I report this encounter to you because this man represents the type of person who concerns me in this book. He poses a threat to the church and the faith. What he said to me at the party was not original or profound. It was more annoying than malicious. You have heard his line before, I'm sure. His attitude is a threat because he is saying to the church and the Christian faith, "Thanks, but I don't need it."

When I meet such people, I'm always tempted to try to outwit them with some caustic comment, some prophetic word which shakes them and devastates their self-satisfied complacency. If I can't convince them or convert them, at least I may be able to insult them! (I have previously confessed to my ministerial temptations.)

What do you say to a person who seems to have it "all together," who claims to have everything he or she needs, who doesn't relate to our presentation of the Christian faith and, what is more, is not bothered by the fact that he or she doesn't relate to the Christian faith? In this chapter I want us to look at this type of person, to focus on two of the statements I heard him, and many others like him, make: "I just don't need it" and "Isn't that what religion is all about?"

That punch-bowl dialogue is a long way from a Nazi death camp, but the two relate to one another. In the darkest days of the Nazi holocaust, a brilliant young theologian looked out of his cell in the Tegel prison and caught a glimpse of the modern world being born. His name was Dietrich Bonhoeffer. Bonhoeffer was a quiet, deeply religious pacifist at the beginning of the war. But because of his deep Christian beliefs, he decided to participate in a plot to assassinate Hitler, convinced that this was the only hope for Germany and the world. The plot failed, and Bonhoeffer was arrested and imprisoned.

Now, in the days before he was to become one of Christianity's modern martyrs, Bonhoeffer not only prayed for, taught, and supported his fellow prisoners, but he also did much thinking about the future of the faith. Sometimes the world's prisoners and victims see the world with the clearest vision. Paul, awaiting death in a Roman prison, saw how feeble are the Caesars of any age. Likewise, Bonhoeffer's vision penetrated the thick walls of his Nazi prison and saw a vision of the threat and promise of the postwar world, a world, in his terms, "come of age," able to solve its own problems.

In his *Letters and Papers from Prison,* Bonhoeffer notes the emergence in our time of "the man of strength." Who is this "man of strength"? He is any strong person, male or female, who is disciplined, ambitious, decent, not overburdened by guilt or self-doubts, responsible, and reasonably generous toward others. While he or she is not hostile toward religion, traditional forms of religiosity and organized religious practices seem to hold little fascination for such a person. Paul Tillich called him a member of "the late Church." He is not "religious"; furthermore, he is not troubled by the fact that he is not religious. Secure, content, competent, reasonably happy and fulfilled, such persons of strength go their own way without any apparent discomfort at having missed the benefits of the Christian faith. In short, they are persons who have strengths and feel no need for what they perceive to be the props of religion.

The person of strength stands in contrast to the person of weakness, the one at the end of one's rope, plagued by guilt, fear, self-doubt, and failure—in short, the person who has needs and knows that he or she has needs.

Bonhoeffer does not claim that the person of strength is a whole person. Such people do have needs, but they are the special needs of the strong. They do have sins, but they are the particular sins of the strong, not the sins of the weak. They do enjoy challenges, but they seem to find their challenges outside the fold of the faith. If the strong ones in our midst are to be made whole, if they are to be fully healed, then, Bonhoeffer says, we must search for new ways to evangelize them. The Good News must be preached to them in a way which sounds like their news for their good.

But what do you give a person who seems to have everything? What do you say to a person who says, through his or her benign neglect of the faith, "Thanks, but I don't need it"? These are the two questions we will occupy ourselves with during the rest of this book.

Bonhoeffer notes that we have traditionally handled strong and joyous persons in our midst by telling them that they are really weak and miserable. We may say something like this: "You may think you have it made. But you are really in a bad predicament, and only we and our message can rescue you." Whenever traditional Christian preaching finds security, it batters away attempting to produce insecurity. When we have come upon people standing on their own two feet, we have tried to bring them to their knees. Our message, as we noted earlier, seems powerless to deliver unless we first devastate. Our evangelism relies on the kind of parent-child relationship which is effective only when we are dealing with immature persons. Only children think that "Father knows best" all the time. So rather than calling people to grow up, we urge them to regress.

No doubt many of these "strong ones" have deep hurts, cares, and an assortment of big and little sins within themselves. In fact, in their strength and maturity they are likely to be more aware of their needs, more candid in admitting them than other less secure people. As we said earlier, truly honest confession comes only from strong people who can dare to be honest. But it seems a bit contrived to insist that they admit to some wretchedness or weakness before they can hear the Good News. Bonhoeffer writes, "When Jesus blessed sinners, they were real sinners, but Jesus did not make every man a sinner first. He called them out of their sin, not into their sin."[1] We do not have to wait until people are at their lowest point in life and have struggled through the "dark night of the soul" to sneak God in the back door of their defenseless hearts. "We should frankly recognize that the world and men have come of age, that we should not speak ill of man in his worldliness, but confront him with God at his strongest point."[2] Why do we, in our evangelism, preaching, witnessing, and theology, tend to aim for people at their weakest points rather than at their strongest?

Even though the Scriptures frequently tell us to "be strong" (1 Corinthians 16:13; Ephesians 6:10; 2 Timothy 2:1; 1 John 2:14), Bonhoeffer notes that too many pastors and Christian apologists ("psychotherapists" and "existentialists," as he calls them) prey upon people's weaknesses and "spy out" the dark secrets of their inner lives in order to "expose their true wretchedness." These efforts to "prey upon the vestigial weaknesses" of mature persons are denounced by Bonhoeffer as poor attempts to turn people back into infants who are in need of dominance and deliverance.

If a person feels neither suffocating guilt nor anguished despair, we try to produce some in order to deliver our Christian package. True, the glory of the Christian faith is, in great part, the glorious account of powerless persons who became empowered, of hungry persons who were filled with good things, of weak persons who became strong, and of guilty persons who were forgiven. But note that such persons are called and helped *out of* their powerlessness, hunger, weakness, and guilt. As Bonhoeffer says, Jesus called people out of, not into, despair: "Never did Jesus throw any doubt on a man's health, vigour or fortune, regarded in themselves, or look upon them as evil fruits. Else why did he heal the sick and restore strength to the weak?"[3] It is true that our self-satisfaction and strengths can be diversions from coming face to face with God. But this is an abuse of strength, not the inherent nature of strength. Our strengths are more than a potentially sinful situation. We have lost the Old Testament category of *blessing* which looks upon strength and prosperity, security and freedom, as gifts of God.

Bonhoeffer disputed the notion that the Bible does not say much about health, fortune, and vigor. Particularly in the Old Testament and scattered throughout the New, we find the assertion that God is the Source of our blessings and strengths, both material and spiritual, that God is divinely concerned with our use of these strengths. The Bible views our strengths as gifts from God and our weaknesses as opportunities for God-given healing and growth. We need a theological perspective which speaks to persons in their strength and prosperity as well as in their weakness and poverty. We need to announce the Good News which, in the words of the old hymn, challenges people "from strength to strength [to] go on."

Our theology must view the strong not as discomforting embarrassments or threats to the faith but as proper recipients of the faith in their strength. We must take seriously the fact that power, strength, maturity, self-discipline, and freedom are not hindrances to living the Christian faith but are gifts to be used gratefully and sacrificially.

First, a theology which speaks to the strong will see gratitude as the foundation of our response to God. Gratitude claims nothing more for itself than its undeserved receiving of gifts. Persons of strength do not have to feign weakness. They do not have to conjure up a false sense of wretchedness or inner despair. They do not have to hide their light under a bushel. They do not have to fake a sense of humility and lowliness. They are gifted. To be "charismatic" (a much-abused word in recent years) is to be, using it in the literal sense of the biblical Greek, a "gifted person." A charismatic person is not necessarily a person who speaks in ecstatic tongues or who has some exotic manifestation of the Spirit. A charismatic person is simply a gifted person. To say this is to affirm that our strengths are not our personal achievements. We are who we are by God's grace (and certain quirks and inequalities of history). There is no such animal as a "self-made man." We must call persons of strength first to be honest about how they got what they have. Call it accident of birth, call it superior advantages, call it fortuitous circumstances, but be sure to call it a *gift*.

The little word "thanks" contains a universe within its boundaries. To say thanks is always to acknowledge something as a gift, to acknowledge that the gift is good, and to acknowledge the existence of a giver. When we say thanks in our table blessings before we eat, we are following the ancient Jewish custom of acknowledging in prayer that food is good, that food comes as a gift, that we cannot survive without such a gift, and that, therefore, we survive because there is a gracious Giver. Pity those who don't feel or express gratitude; pity them for what they don't know about themselves, their lives, or their God.

What does God want from us? Nothing more, nothing less than thanks—thanksgiving expressed in our words and lives.

Second, a theology of strength does not say that strong persons with their God-given talents and strengths are without any needs of their own. They have their gifts. They also have their needs. But let us remember that they have a particular set of needs. As we noted earlier, one reason that our message to the strong falls upon deaf ears is that we accuse them of sins which they don't have, recommend cures for sicknesses with which they are not infected, and offer comfort for pain they don't feel. They have their needs and their sins; but they are the needs and the sins of the strong, not the weak.

What are some of the "sins of the strong"? Self-righteousness, complacency, pretensions of self-sufficiency and omnipotence, failure to empathize with weaker brothers and sisters—to name a few. These are the sins which infect people who have strengths but who suffer from a paucity of thankfulness and a deficiency of gratitude. They are the sins of anyone who says (as my friend at the punch bowl said), "Well, I'm happy, contented, well fed, reasonably decent; and, after all, isn't that what religion is all about?"

No, that isn't "what religion is all about." In fact, it's just the opposite. Many of the strong share with the weak the erroneous notion that self-fulfillment, self-gratification, and self-sufficiency are the only goals of religion. For some pagan religions, such self-centeredness is the goal. For Christianity, it is not. Our Lord tells us that if we want to find ourselves, we must lose ourselves in something greater than ourselves. In giving ourselves to others, we receive back the true selves that we were created to be.

But who can blame people for concluding that their self-contentment is "what religion is all about"? We present the Christian faith as "the best deal a person ever had," as the payoff in blessings for our good deeds, as a panacea for all our personal aches and pains. If a person already has health, happiness, a reasonable amount of joy, and a passable sense of contentment, then it's easy for that person to assume that he or she already possesses all the benefits of the Christian faith and, therefore, has nothing else to gain by dabbling in religion. The assumption is incorrect but nonetheless understandable, considering the way we usually present the faith.

Persons of strength do have needs, and one of their most pressing needs is a need to be challenged beyond the narrow confines of their limited notions of both their own lives and the Christian faith. Many strong persons, because they have the resources to handle more of the everyday problems which bedevil weaker souls, think they have the strength to handle *every* problem. Their strength blinds them to their weaknesses. This, I think, is why Jesus said that it was as difficult for a rich man to enter the kingdom of God as for an elephant to be comfortable in a Toyota. It is difficult simply because the rich, who can solve most of life's nitty-gritty problems through their checkbooks, delude themselves into thinking that they can solve *all* of life's difficulties in this manner. The rich fool whom Jesus told about was called a fool because he thought that his money insured him against the vicissitudes of human existence. The poor are "blessed," not because material or spiritual poverty makes life more fun, but because the poor are less apt to indulge themselves in the self-deception and false sense of security which riches often engender. "Blessed are the poor" because they are more likely to catch on to the fact of our basic dependency upon a gracious God.

Many people whose lives are spent gaining more power in such areas as education, business, and politics will always feel weak because they can never get enough power to be satisfied. Many rich people will always feel destitute because they can never get enough money to be satisfied. A materialistic, consumptive society such as ours will invariably be an impoverished society, always getting but never getting enough, losing as much as it gains, destroying all the time when it thinks it is building.

This is the hard note of judgment which must be heard by persons of strength. If you think that I'm advocating a new bourgeois theology to bless our mad acquisition of things and our irresponsible appropriation of power, you are mistaken. We must tell the strong ones in our midst that their strength, when misdirected, is weakness. The poverty of the poor is tragic; so is the peculiar poverty of the rich. The intellectual can never know enough. The scholar will perish whether she or he publishes or not. The businessperson climbs to the top of the organizational pecking order only to find that, rather than running the business, it now runs him or her. The preacher compromises along the way to the episcopacy only to find that, as bishop, there is nothing left to say. The more money we acquire for ourselves, the less we have on which to spend it. We must be able to see the starvation behind the faces of Amos's "fat cows of Bashan."

Please note, to refer you back to the first point of this book, that we can speak with particularly prophetic judgment on the sins and needs of the strong because we first recognize their strengths and call those strengths gifts of God. Strong people are gifted, blessed, fortunate individuals. Their strengths are opportunities, not hindrances. There is no reason why the faith cannot be lived as well by the five-talent person as by the two-talent person. (You recall that in Jesus's parable of the talents, the more talented people did more to multiply and use their talents than did the less talented people!) Riches are not evil in themselves. They are dangerous, but not inherently evil. Our strengths are gifts and, like any gift, can be used for good or ill. Once again, we begin by speaking of grace and then move on to speak of judgments and responsibilities. Gratitude is a much more productive motivation for discipleship than abasement.

What do you give a strong person who seems to have everything? One thing you can give him or her is a new perspective on his or her strength. You give a challenge. You give an opportunity to see those strengths as gifts from God. You give the freedom to use those strengths for something greater than one's own selfish desires. Conversion (*metanoia*, turning around, change of life and heart) for the person of strength would involve, not a denial of strengths, but rather the kind of humbling gratitude which comes when one realizes that one's gifts have a divine source and purpose. To be gifted, from a Christian perspective, is to be held responsible for the use of those gifts. "To whom much is given, of him shall much be required."

Out there on the Damascus Road, Paul found his strength transformed by the love of God. He found his particular need met by a particular challenge. Paul discovered that he, as a man of wisdom and strength, was, in reality, a slave held in bondage to such things as earthly wisdom, temporal success, pride, and constant business. Paul found that what the world calls strong is not always strong. His strength was transformed by the Source of true strength. He heard the call (for Paul never speaks of a "conversion") to a life which used all of his intellect, all of his education, all of his physical and emotional strength. Paul, by his own claim, was a man who had everything, everything except a knowledge of where his giftedness came from and something important for which to use his giftedness. That's what he got on the Damascus Road.

Jesus showed us true strength. He showed us that real strength lies in having so much power within oneself that one is free to be carefree with power, to give power away, to "empty oneself." He who knows the value of life is the one who is able to give up life for others. The one who is master of all is the one who is able to be servant of all. The one who is richest is the one who knows how limited are our checkbooks in helping us to solve our deepest yearnings. The one who is most liberated is the one who yokes oneself to the plight of the oppressed.

Let us speak to persons of strength with a challenge which shakes them to the core with its boldness. As Christians, as the church, we have demanded so little. We have spoken of Christianity as if it were a cushion and not a cross. We have promised to relieve people of all their aches and pains, all their cares and burdens, all their questions and doubts. We have transformed the faith into an insipid soufflé with all air and no nourishment, a sweet placebo which cures nothing because it challenges no one. It is a faith which is hardly worth living for, much less dying for. We have so tamed and housebroken the Spirit that it soothes more than it prods. This dull, domesticated, impotent version of the faith is a heresy which mocks the Christianity for which people once bled. We need people who can present the Christian faith, by their words and deeds, in such a way that everyone grows stronger and taller having encountered them. The recovery of our old, holy boldness is that for which we must now pray.

Nazi Germany. Easter week of 1945. American artillery thunders on a collapsing Western Front. Hitler, growing more insane as the end of the Third Reich draws near, orders the quick executions of a number of notable political prisoners, particularly those who participated in the abortive resistance movement.

At Schönberg, on Low Sunday, Dietrich Bonhoeffer leads his fellow prisoners in a morning worship service. Even though they know that the end of their lives must be near, an atmosphere of courage and hope permeates the service. They find themselves, in this deep hour of need, leaning on Bonhoeffer, who seems to be a perpetual source of courage and strength. Bonhoeffer reads from 1 Peter 1:3: "Blessed be the God and Father of our Lord Jesus Christ! By his great mercy we have been born anew to a living hope through the resurrection of Jesus Christ from the dead." Bonhoeffer then speaks of the meaning of these ancient words for their present situation. Payne Best, an imprisoned English officer, later recalls how Bonhoeffer's strength and religious faith sustained all the prisoners that day. Just as Bonhoeffer finishes the last prayer, the door of the cell bursts open, and two sinister men enter and say, "Prisoner Bonhoeffer, get ready to come with us."

Everyone knows what this means. As Bonhoeffer leaves the room, he whispers to one fellow prisoner, "This is the end. . . . For me the beginning of life." He is then taken away.

On the cold, gray dawn of Monday, April 9, 1945, Dietrich Bonhoeffer—brilliant theologian, biblical scholar, ethicist, teacher, poet, son of a noble family of German intellectuals—becomes a martyr and is hanged until dead at Flossenbürg.[4]

The Nazis did not know, could not know, that within the death of this one good and strong man their inevitable defeat was being accomplished. Bonhoeffer had everything: intelligence, material things, fame, inner discipline, and strength. But above all these things, he had heard a challenge, a challenge which he would live and die by. He had a Christlike faith which freed him to ask the toughest of questions and risk the boldest of deeds. His light was so strong that the darkness could not quench it; indeed, the darker the night, the more brightly his light shone.

Dietrich Bonhoeffer had heard the call of Christ in accents so strong and clear that he brought the realm of darkness and evil to its knees, even while it thought it was bringing him to his.

From Whom All Blessings Flow

6

From the Nazi death camp in the twentieth century, I take you to a house church in Rome in the third century. A group of people stand around a simple wooden table. In that gathering are men—slaves, nobles, people from different races and cultures. Now these former distinctions do not matter, for they are all Christians—"One in Christ," as they say. Many who stand there show the scars of torture by government authorities, scars which they now bear as privileged signs of their faithfulness.

They gather secretly in the dining room of a large private home on Sunday, under threat of persecution by the government, to celebrate a common religious meal they call the "Eucharist" (the "thanksgiving". A large man stands at the head of the table with hands upraised in prayer, He, like the other worshipers, wears the usual Roman street clothes of the day. They call him an *Episcopos* ("Bishop" or "Superintendent") and have given him the responsibility of overseeing the life of the congregation, helping them care for the poor, and leading them in the Eucharist.

The assembly has just completed prayers, chanted a couple of psalms, and had a long Scripture reading and sermon by the *Episcopos*, followed by the worshipers embracing one another in the "kiss of peace." Now "The Gifts" are called forth. The people bring forward little loaves of bread, a large two-handled cup, and jugs of wine. The bread and wine have come from the homes of the worshipers; they bring them as their offering for the Eucharist. The *deakonoi* ("deacons" or "waiters") gather the bread and wine and present them to the *Episcopos*, who says in a loud voice: "Lift up your hearts!"

"We lift them up to the Lord!" respond the people in one voice.

Then the *Episcopos*, standing behind the table with the elders of the congregation and all the people gathered around the table, raises his hands and offers a blessing over The Gifts:

We give thanks *(eucharistia)* unto You, O God, through Your Beloved Child Jesus Christ, Whom in the last times You sent to us as a Saviour and Redeemer and the Messenger of Your counsel; Who is your Word inseparable from You, through Whom You made all things and in Whom You were well-pleased; Whom You sent from heaven unto the Virgin's womb and Who conceived within her was made flesh and demonstrated to be your Son being born of Holy Spirit and a Virgin; Who fulfilling Your will and preparing for You a holy people stretched forth His hands for suffering that He might release from sufferings those who have believed in You:

Who when He was betrayed to voluntary suffering that He might abolish death and rend the bonds of the devil and tread down hell and enlighten the righteous and establish the ordinance and demonstrate the resurrection: Taking bread and giving thanks to You said: Take, eat: this is My Body which is broken for you. Likewise also the cup, saying: This is My Blood which is shed for you. When you do this, you do My remembrance.

Doing therefore the remembrance of His death and resurrection, we offer to You the bread and the cup, making thanksgiving to You because You have bidden us to stand before You and minister as priests to You. And we pray You that You would grant to all who partake to be united that they may be fulfilled with the Holy Spirit for the confirmation of faith in truth, that we may praise and glorify You through Your Child Jesus Christ through whom be glory and honour unto You with the Holy Spirit in Your holy Church now and world without end. Amen.[1]

"Amen!" shout all the worshipers at the end of the prayer of thanksgiving.

The *Episcopos* breaks the bread and asks all to come forward to eat and drink. The bread and wine are passed around the circle of worshipers until each person has partaken of the Eucharist.

"Amen!" say the people at the end of the concluding prayer.

"Go in peace!" says the *Episcopos.*

They go out into a hostile world in which some of them may have to pay a high price for their faith. But they will gladly pay it because, in their worship, they have experienced the rewarding fellowship with a New Lord and a New People in a New Age.

How this early scene contrasts with our usually somber, lifeless worship of today! The typical Protestant worship service is too much talk and too little action. It consists mainly in a preacher-choir performance in which the congregation comes either to be entertained or scolded, titillated or berated. There are prayers filled with vague, empty phrases and meaningless clichés. The cold, stiff, impersonal atmosphere is penetrated occasionally by insipid, anachronistic hymns. The tone is heavy on the penitence and confession and weak on the celebration. No wonder that in recent years there has been a veritable revolution in Christian worship—not necessarily because we desire something new and "way-out" when we worship (although some have tried this, too), but because we want to recover some of the ancient feeling of worship as the praise of God! This is an experience we seem to have lost.

To refer to earlier chapters, the root problem with our worship is much the same problem which we have with our preaching and evangelism: we have lost the sense of the Good News about the God who has done something, is doing something, and will continue to do something in our behalf. Our worship has become a rather feeble attempt to "get right with God." In many churches worship has degenerated into little more than psychological manipulation in which the architecture, the lighting and decoration, the words of the preacher, and the music of the choir are all carefully orchestrated to induce an appropriate feeling in the worshipers. Many secure, thinking people are repulsed by this subtle Sunday morning attempt at manipulation by artificial means. The worship designers may be trying to get the congregation to make a "decision for Christ" or to motivate them for "social action" or to put them in a spiritual dream world which takes their minds off the real world. The point is that the whole worship service is designed on the basis of what it is supposed to do for the worshipers, not on the basis of some kind of relationship with God.

When I do workshops in local churches on worship renewal, I often use an analogy which Kierkegaard once used in writing about worship. Kierkegaard said that he might think of the worship in our churches on Sunday morning as if it were a drama taking place in a theater. So I draw a theater floor plan on a chalkboard with the stage at one end and the audience at the other end. Then I ask people to list on the theater plan all the participants in a usual Sunday morning worship service. They usually list the worship participants in an arrangement something like the diagram on this page. With nearly every group in which I have used this analogy, this is the way the drama of worship is arranged. There is only one problem. Where is God? We have left God out of worship! We have set up worship as if it were a performance by the "actors" (minister, choir, etc.) for the sole benefit of the "audience" (congregation). In this scheme, the only way to judge the effectiveness of worship is to judge how well the congregation likes it. And that is usually how we judge worship.

The Worship Theater

Minister Choir Organist/Choir Leader Acolytes Ushers	Stage
Congregation	Audience

Let's change the arrangement in The Worship Theater so that it looks like this:

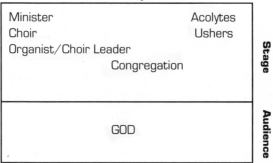

Now that changes things. God is brought into the worship service! This arrangement says that most of the singing, praying, talking, washing, eating, and drinking which we do on Sunday morning is addressed to God, not to ourselves. The true measure of worship is not so much what it does to or for us. The true test is what worship says to and about God. Too many of our public prayers seem to be sermonettes with the eyes closed, in which the congregation is exhorted to do this or think that, rather than attempts to communicate with the divine. Adoration, mystery, awe, wonder, sacrifice, offering, thanksgiving, and praise are often missing from our public worship because we have made ourselves, rather than God, the object of our worship.

Our worship will never again be "celebration" in any important sense of the word until we recover an important object of celebration. The celebration of ourselves or humanity in general or other vague platitudes like love, joy, liberation, and peace is not enough. W. H. Auden's tongue-in-cheek prayer is too real to be funny:

O God, put away justice and truth for we cannot understand them and do not want them. Eternity would bore us dreadfully. Leave Thy heavens and come down to our earth of waterclocks and hedges. Become our uncle.

Look after Baby, amuse Grandfather, escort Madam to the Opera, help Willy with his homework, introduce Muriel to a handsome naval officer. Be interesting and weak like us, and we will love you as we love ourselves.[2]

Paul exhorts us to give thanks continually "*in the name of our Lord Jesus Christ*" (Ephesians 5:20, italics added), to give thanks "to God the Father *through him*" (Colossians 3:17, italics added). He tells the Romans, "I thank my God *through Jesus Christ for all of you*" (Romans 1:8, italics added). The words "in" and "through" are important; for only in and by Christ, who has atoned for our ingratitude, can we show true gratitude. If we focused more upon God, if our worship became a song of our beliefs about God, if it again became a response to the working out of our salvation by the One who truly heals us, then we would have something to sing about! The Germans speak of worship as *Gottesdienst*, "God's service." In using this term, from the little I know of German Reformed theology, they mean not only the service which we render to God when we worship but also the service of God to us. In other words, they are focusing on the mighty acts by which God has reached out to us through Jesus Christ. They are speaking first about what God has done rather than about what we should be doing. That early prayer which the *Episcopos* prayed over The Gifts at the Eucharist was a prayer of thanksgiving (*eucharistia*) in which the bread and the wine were blessed by thankfully recalling all the great events of our salvation history. Our worship is our acknowledgment of what God has done for us. As Barth said, it is simply our rendering—in prayer, sermon, act, and song—of our human "Thanks."

The Lord's Supper, or Eucharist ("thanks"), is the central act of Christian worship not only because Jesus instituted it and asked us to continue it but also because it is our thanksgiving, our response in bread and wine, prayer and song, to what has been done for us in Christ. Gratitude is the basis of praise, which is the basis of joyful, celebrative worship. Could the reason much of our worship (especially in middle-class white congregations) is dull and lifeless be that (1) we have forgotten the old story of our salvation history and therefore have forgotten who we are ("a royal priesthood . . ."), and (2) we have forgotten that God is the Source of all our strengths and blessings and therefore the object of our greatest shouts of praise, and (3) we are not inclined to praise God for anything so basic and material as our families, our homes, our education, our talents, and our food? Gratitude makes artists of us all, asking us to fashion our lives more fittingly into the offerings of praise and thanksgiving which they are called to be. When we lay the bread, wine, and money on the altar in worship, we lay not only our material creations which are the gifts of God's creation, but we are also laying ourselves upon the altar. As Paul Tillich once noted, "Thanksgiving is consecration; it transfers something that belongs to the secular world into the sphere of the holy."[3] The offering is not a "collection"; it is not "paying our dues"; it is not an intrusion into a sweet service of worship. The offering is what we are about when we worship.

If you compare the new liturgies for the Lord's Supper or Holy Communion among Roman Catholics, Lutherans, Episcopalians, United Methodists, Presbyterians, and the United Church of Christ with what these groups were saying at the Lord's Supper in years past, you will see a dramatic change of tone and emphasis in their worship. That change of tone is brought about, in great part, because we have discovered that the Lord's Supper is more than a somber memorial, a doleful lamentation for the death of Jesus. The Lord's Supper is not the Last Supper. The Last Supper was the sorrowful gathering of Jesus and the disciples before the crucifixion. The Lord's Supper celebrates, not the Last Supper, but the Emmaus supper—the supper which Jesus ate with his disciples after his resurrection victory. At Emmaus their eyes were opened, and Jesus was made known to them in the breaking of the bread. It was a joyful meal because their whole situation had changed. The new age had dawned. As Henry Sloane Coffin once remarked, "You can't have a funeral without a corpse." We Christians don't have a corpse. Our Lord is risen; a sad, doleful, funeral meal is inappropriate to our changed human condition.

We are Easter people! Every Sunday worship service is a little Easter, a time when we die and rise with Jesus again. That's why we Christians do not observe or worship on the Jewish sabbath. We worship on Sunday, the day of the Resurrection, to emphasize that Christ has made all things new, including us! Every Sunday is Easter Sunday.

That's what the disciples of John the Baptist couldn't understand about the behavior of Jesus and his disciples. (We noted in an earlier chapter how the preaching of John differed from the preaching of Jesus.) John's people wondered why Jesus's disciples did not fast. "Why fast?" Jesus replied. "You fast if you are sorrowful. My disciples have something to be happy about. The guests at a wedding party are not in mourning. They are joyful because the bridegroom is with them. I am here! Eat, drink, and be merry."

We must restore that joyful responsiveness to our worship. The place to start is with the Lord's Supper since it is biblically and historically the central act of Christian worship. The Pharisees' charge that Jesus was a glutton and a wine-bibber is well-documented in the Gospel accounts. Jesus liked parties. John says that his first miracle was the turning of water into wine so that the wedding party could continue. He ate and drank with sinners; he fed the multitude; he invited all to the feast; he sought to fill all the spiritually and physically hungry people with good things.

As I said in a recent sermon of mine which appeared in John Killinger's book *The Eleven O'clock News*:

Worship means to serve God. That's why you call it a "service" of worship. Now there are basically two ways to serve God. One is to run errands for him—feed the hungry, love the poor, fight on his side, and the like. The other way to serve him is to do things that you need to do because he is God and you are one of his children. Like singing songs for him, laughing for him, shedding a tear for him, telling him what's on your mind. In general, it is to rejoice and make a fool of yourself for him the way lovers have always made fools of themselves for somebody they love. There's always got to be a little joy and a little foolishness at any good party, and the same goes for the party that takes place here each Sunday. One thing I'm sure of, God wants us to have a good time. I'm sure of that—good times, good news, good God.[4]

The somber black robes which many of our clergy wear might need to be exchanged for brighter liturgical vestments. Our sanctuaries could be more appropriately decorated with banners, brighter lights, color. Our hymns need to be evaluated with close attention paid to what they say and how they are sung. Our liturgies and prayers need to say more about who God is, what God has done and is doing, and who we are because of who God is. Our sermons must become more bold, more biblical, more engaging. Our worship must become a *cantis firmis* for our deliverance, our challenge, our commission. We should leave each worship service refreshed, renewed, strengthened, marching forth—with banners flying—into the world to be about our Father's business. *How* we worship is not as important as *what* we worship. If we can become more explicit and sure of whom and what we worship, the how of worship will evolve naturally.

Driving along a rural road in North Carolina, I passed two little churches with signs in front of each church. PREPARE TO MEET THY GOD, read the sign at the first church. SING A NEW SONG UNTO THE LORD, read the sign at the second church. There you have the difference between much of our traditional worship, on the one hand—worship which deals in threats, obligations, payoffs, psychological manipulations, and attempts to "get right with God"—and, on the other hand, our current attempt to recover our earlier worship, which is worship as a response to a gracious God. Someday I'm going back and worship at that second church. I'll wager that those folk know how to worship because they know *whom* to worship!

To Whom Much Is Given

The story is told of a little tribe of Indians who lived long ago in Mississippi. The tribe lived near a swift river, a river in which the current was so strong and deadly that no person could cross without being swept downstream and drowned.

Then came the day when another tribe of hostile Indians attacked the village. The Indians were soon fighting with their backs to the river. They couldn't move anywhere except into the swift river. They knew that their only hope was to try to cross. So they gathered the youngest and oldest members of their tribe. The strong ones placed these weaker ones on their shoulders, and they risked wading into the river. Amazingly, the weight of their fellow tribespeople on their shoulders kept them from losing their footing, and they were able to cross the swift stream and escape without harm.

This little story sums up, at the beginning, what I wish to say in this chapter. Here I want to speak about people who are so strong that they are able to carry other people's weight besides their own.

"Only he who is already loved can love; only he who has been trusted can trust; only he who has been an object of devotion can give himself." Thus, the great German theologian Rudolf Bultmann reminds us that Christian ethics, the mode of Christian action, is our response to the gracious love of God. As a young theology student at Oxford, John Wesley earnestly wanted to be a good Christian. He founded the "Holy Club" which imposed rigorous self-discipline and strict performance of good works upon its members. But Wesley's good works and high conduct gave him little joy. John and his brother Charles traveled across England to visit the great divine, William Law, who told them that they were trying to make something complicated and burdensome out of the simple blessing of Christianity. "Religion is the plainest and simplest thing in the world," Law told the two earnest young men. "It is just this: 'We love, because he first loved us'" (1 John 4:19).

There you have it. When Christians do good things, they do them not to get anywhere; they do them because they have already arrived. As we said in the last chapter, all God wants from us is thanks. That is the reason we sing (worship), and that is also the reason we work (ethics).

There is a vast difference between the ethics of achievement and the ethics of response. Christian ethics is more than an attempt to "do good," for, as Luther found, our doing good is just one more misdirected attempt to win God over to our side when, all along, God is on our side! Christian ethics is more than a noble humanitarian gesture. The object of humanitarian love is humanity. The humanitarian usually loves on the basis of what he or she perceives to be the "loveworthiness" of humanity. But sometimes humanity is not so attractive. Sometimes humanity, because of its inhumanity, seems most unworthy of being loved by anybody. The Christian does not love his or her neighbor because the neighbor is a nice person or because the neighbor deserves love or because the neighbor returns love; the Christian loves in response to the love with which God has loved him or her. The Christian loves first because of what she or he believes about God, not because of something she or he believes about humanity. That is why Christian love is often more persistent and more radical than mere humanitarian love. Christian love is more than a feeling. We have already spoken of how notoriously fickle feelings are. Nowhere in the Bible is love defined as a feeling. Love, in the biblical sense, is an activity, a decision, a response, something you decide to do because of what you know about God.

Once again, this is why we must always proclaim grace first, not second. You can't beat people on the head, bring them to their knees, devastate their human dignity, and then expect them to act like mature, responsible, full human beings. What a Christian does comes from the incredible assumption that there can be no serious discussion of what a person ought to be doing without a prior serious discussion of what a person is. As Harry Emerson Fosdick used to say, "*Oughtness* . . . is essentially related to *isness*."[1] Morals cannot be divorced from religion because while morals deal with what people *ought* to do and be, religion is basically a message about what people *are*. The Christian faith says that people are not helpless lambs, that they are not the scum of the earth, that they are not the accidental by-products of a chemical reaction in the cosmos; they are children of God who have been created and delivered from estrangement, despair, guilt, slavery, and weakness. The Christian faith asks of people, "Seeing that we have this great gift, shall we not do this or that in celebration and response to God?"

Our message to the strong ones in our midst must affirm that true strength comes from the confidence of knowing who they really are. True strength comes not from the rock-hard, self-centered, and self-sufficient facade put up by some so-called strong people; rather, true strength comes from the God-given confidence and grace of knowing their secure place in the good heart of God.

We must call people to the ethically responsible use of their strengths. But the church seems to have problems with that. People today are suspicious of power and strength. Some Christian thinkers, like William Stringfellow and Jacques Ellul, identify power with the sins of Babylon, content to make the rather elementary assertion that power corrupts. Power does corrupt. But, as Richard Neuhaus points out, it is despicable for us to condemn the strength of others as being unredeemably immoral while we exercise power in our blanket condemnations of the power of others! We tend to back off from the dilemma of power and talk more about personal sins, sins of weakness, and individual problems rather than tackling the tough questions about corporate sinfulness, ethically responsible use of power, and stewardship of our gifts. It is not enough for us to tell businesspersons that the business world is prone to substitute profit for ethics. It is not enough for us to tell rich people that money is dangerous. It is not enough for us to tell American white middle-class people that they live in a nation which tends to victimize other nations with its imperialistic power. We must go on to speak about how one might respond faithfully even in circumstances of strength.

After a recent sermon of mine on "World Famine as a Christian Concern," an exasperated lay person met me at the church door and said, "All you've done is to make me feel guilty that my family has enough to eat. I can't help that. You told me nothing that I could do to help a man in India keep his family from starving. Tell me how to do that, and I'll get busy." Obviously, I had failed to get beyond simplistic, preacherly scolding and guilt building. Such preaching is less than the gospel.

As we have often been reminded, power corrupts and absolute power corrupts absolutely. But must the educated, rich, and influential persons (for I must remind you that compared to the vast majority of our brothers and sisters in the world, nearly all Americans are rich, educated, and influential) forsake their gifts in order to enter the kingdom? We must do more than quit our jobs and move to an agricultural commune in Vermont. We must do more than wistfully long for the supposed innocence of the powerless. We must do more than proclaim reductionistic, naive platitudes about power. Rather, we must deal with the hard task of thinking about how to use power in a responsible way. For most of us have been blessed in special ways. Some of our gifts have come from God; some of them have come from our own selfish exploitation and mad striving. Now, what will we do with those gifts?

The ethical responsibility to which we call the person of strength takes the stress off rules and regulations. Mere legalistic rules may not be demanding enough. Rules foster irresponsibility since, once we have kept the law, we feel we have no other responsibility. On the other hand, an ethic of responsibility has no terminus; it knows infinite responsibility to all persons because it is infinitely responsible to God. "To whom much is given, of him will much be required" (Luke 12:48b). How trivial of us to encapsulate Christian morals into petty individual codes of personal behavior rather than to demand the kind of ethical boldness which Jesus demonstrated! We must rise above Nietzsche's charge that Christianity fosters a mere "slave morality." When the rich young ruler came to Jesus, he asked Jesus, "What must I do to inherit eternal life?" Jesus told him to obey the rules. "I already do that," the young man responded. "Then go sell everything you have, and give it to the poor," Jesus said. Jesus was not laying down a new rule (though we should probably take this command of Jesus more seriously than we usually take it); Jesus was simply offering the young man a way to live, not by the limits of rules and regulations, but by the freedom and challenge of responsible gratitude.

In our talk about Christian ethics, we must offer the strong, in the words of Dana Prom Smith in *The Debonaire Disciple*, an ethical stance which is "less a matter of rules or codes of conduct than of guides in gratitude."[2] Smith recalls that when a child misbehaves, a father can either lay down the law in an attempt to coerce the child into goodness or sit down on the edge of the bed at night and talk to the child about what counts in life and about how much his father and mother love him and believe in him. Laying down the law may make the father feel powerful, but it will render the child into either a docile little lamb who is incapable of deciding things for himself or into a hostile reactionary who spends his life not thinking about what he should do but about how he can rebel against his father's laying down the law. Gratitude, not obligation, is at the heart of the matter.

Children seek rules, black and white codes of conduct, simplistic canons of what is always right and what is always wrong. Children seek rules; mature adults need challenges. The person of strength will be urged to ask, "What is God asking of me in the light of my God-given talents and abilities and in the light of my neighbor's needs?" We are accountable for our talents and our gifts. To tell a person of strength that self-discipline, creativity, competence, and intellect should be smothered under the cloak of imitative weakness would be like telling him or her to go bury his or her talents in a field.

Throughout the Bible prosperous persons are entrusted with great responsibility. The poor are always the responsibility of the rich. (By the way, in the Bible to be "rich" simply means anyone who owns something, has a roof over one's head and enough food to get by from day to day.) In the Bible it is not the responsibility of the widows and orphans to fend for themselves. There is no debate in the Bible about the "deserving poor." There is often talk about the "undeserving rich" but not the "deserving or undeserving poor." The poor are the responsibility of the rich simply because the poor are poor and powerless and the rich are rich and powerful. We, who live in the part of the world which controls 80 percent of the world's resources (a country where less than one-fifth of the world's population consumes one-half of the world's resources), need to hear that call to responsibility.

A recent television advertisement shows a young paperboy delivering his newspapers after school. The advertisement, which is presented by an oil company as a "public service," goes something like this: "You are looking at a businessman. He works only a few hours after school each day. But this little businessman makes more money each day than over three-fourths of all the world's people. Free Enterprise—it works." Who are we kidding? The history of our country, the nature of our geographical and geological situation tells us that we are where we are not necessarily because this or that business system works better than some other system, but because we have been richly blessed and we have been aggressively self-seeking. If a young paperboy, working after school on a paper route, can make more money than three-fourths of the world's hard-working men and women, what does that say to us about the just distribution of the gifts of the earth?

How are prosperous persons to be responsible as their brother's keepers and as God's stewards? I am confident that the answers to that question will come as we start to see ourselves for who we are—people of gifts and people of responsibilities. Thank God that the good Samaritan had money, and thank God that the good Samaritan responded to the need of his neighbor with his money. Our response doesn't have to be merely in individual terms. Think how the story might have turned out if the Samaritan's neighbor had been a neighborhood. Think of how many ways we have in our modern world for responding not just to individual neighbors but to whole neighborhoods as well. We in the "have" nations have unique opportunities to help the "have nots" of the world. We are fortunate enough to have been born into a community of doers and deciders. Our skills and gifts require us to make difficult decisions each day. We are not helpless in the face of the cruelties in life. A person in India may be concerned about the starving child in South America. But aside from prayer, there is little that the Indian can do. The case is different for us.

Many of our traditional prayers and collects which we used to pray stress the omnipotence of God and the helplessness of humanity:

> "Almighty God, who seest that we have no power of
>   ourselves to help ourselves . . ."
> "Through the weakness of our mortal nature, we can do
>   no good without thee . . ."

Is that really our present situation? We may be helpless in an ultimate sense. There are still many areas of our lives over which we do not have control. But we are far from totally helpless. Our competence to solve many of humanity's age-old problems is growing. Can we respond out of this relative, but nevertheless real, human competence?

Strong people, who are not only materially strong but emotionally and spiritually strong as well, are people who have unique opportunities for Christian response in significant ways. The immature, weak person is fragmented and enslaved by immediate concerns, conflicting loyalties, and the approval of others. The great needs and tough questions of the modern world demand mature, integrated, disciplined Christians who have a Source of strength which is greater than the world gives. These are the tough ones, willing to let others lean on them, willing to have their strength used by someone else who may not be as strong. Such strength can be an instrument, not a hindrance, to the achievement of social justice and human liberation. Let us call upon the strong ones among us to rise from strength to greater strength and take responsibility for their places in the history of salvation. They must use their talents and not just feel guilty or run away from wrestling with their responsibilities. Only such strong persons have the kind of inner strength and freedom which permits them, in Luther's words, to "sin boldly," to give themselves away freely to something greater than themselves, to risk bold and decisive deeds in behalf of their neighbors.

It is a psychological axiom that only secure, strong persons have the freedom to love others selflessly. It takes a well-endowed person to be truly selfless and gracious. Eric Fromm, in *The Art of Loving*, contrasts the person who keeps with the person who gives:

> The most widespread misunderstanding is that which assumes that giving is "giving up" something, being deprived of, sacrificing. People whose main orientation is a nonproductive one feel giving as an impoverishment. . . .
>
> For the productive character, giving has an entirely different meaning. Giving is the highest expression of potency. In the very act of giving, I experience my strength, my wealth, my power. . . . I experience myself as overflowing, spending, alive, hence as joyous. Giving is more joyous than receiving, not because it is a deprivation, but because in the act of giving lies the expression of my aliveness.[3]

The giving of the strong is the giving of responsible, responsive, gifted people.

The love of the weak person usually comes from the insecurity of self-disparagement or from guilt. Such love is not given out of strength and wholeness. It is love which comes from guilt or the attempts of "works righteousness," not from freedom and gratitude. Too often such love is subtle selfishness in which things are done in order to get other things. One seeks compensation or expiation; hence, one can never do enough, and, hence, one smothers the other person with solicitude. The Blacks have been right in recent years to point out that the love of many white liberals is either degradingly patronizing or is a love which attempts to make some claim on its recipients. It is, therefore, selfish love which comes not from the graciousness of strength but, rather, from the weakness of white guilt. Genuine Christian love is selfless. Pagan love is the love which loves in an attempt to achieve some sort of self-gratification. Christian love gives without expectation of return or even any need for being returned. Only the strong, secure person has the freedom to love the neighbor as oneself, allowing the neighbor freedom and dignity.

A Parable

I t was my friend Clayton's fourth birthday. And because four years old is a very special age, his mother told him that he could have any kind of birthday party he wished.

"I want a party where everybody there will be kings and queens," Clayton replied without a moment's hesitation. His wish was granted. His mother started to work, creating a score of golden paper crowns, royal blue crepe paper robes with gold lining, and scepters made from coat hangers and cardboard. Then the afternoon of the party came. As the guests arrived, they were delighted to receive royal crowns, robes, and scepters. Everyone at the party was either a king or queen. And everyone had a wonderful time at Clayton's party. All the guests enjoyed cake and ice cream. They had a majestic procession up to the end of the block and back. All looked like kings and queens. All believed they were kings and queens. Moreover, they all *acted* like kings and queens. They all behaved in a most regal manner.

That night, when the guests had all gone home, when the cake and ice cream had been cleared away and Clayton was being tucked into bed by his mother, Clayton said, "I wish *everyone* in the whole world could be a king or a queen—not just on my birthday, but *everybody*."

Well, Clayton, something very much like that happened two thousand years ago at a place called Calvary. We, who were nobodies, became somebodies. If we could all believe that, perhaps we could start *acting* like that.

You are a chosen race, a royal priesthood, a dedicated nation, and a people claimed by God for his own, to proclaim the triumphs of him who has called you out of darkness into his marvellous light. You are now the people of God, who once were not his people; outside his mercy once, you have now received his mercy. (1 Peter 2:9–10, NEB)

Strength in Numbers

8

I think it was the poet Shelley who said, "I could believe in Christ if he did not drag along with him that leprous bride of his—the church." Shelley's problem with the church is neither novel nor his problem alone. If the church is "the bride of Christ," as some optimistic biblical writers claimed, then she has been an unfaithful bride whose fidelity scarcely lasted through the honeymoon.

In recent years, there has been a plethora of criticism of the church, most of it well deserved. Membership declines in mainline Protestant denominations, shrinking church attendance and giving, and the loss of many youth are all part of the sad statistical story. A score of books has documented the lethargy and the hypocrisy of the contemporary church which has become a baptizer of comfortable, white, middle-class values, virtually indistinguishable in program and creed from the local garden club.

Now granting that much of this criticism is valid, granting that those of us in the church must honestly face it (in fact, the most severe and penetrating critics of the church are often those on the inside who love it the most), let us also be honest about some of the reasons why some people do not like the church. The charge that the church cannot and will not change for the better is indefensible. Few institutions in our society have undergone such rigorous self-examination or have changed as much in as short a time as the church. Think, for instance, of how radically the venerable old Roman Catholic church changed after Vatican II. It changed more in the past ten years than it had in the past five hundred. The recent changes in attitudes and programs among many denominations, when compared with defensive and reactionary organizations like the American Bar Association or the American Medical Association, show that the church is neither as rigid nor as backward as its critics have claimed. No, much of this contemporary criticism of the church has deeper roots.

In this chapter I contend that many people's dislike of the church stems not from their disappointment that the church has failed to be what she is called to be but, rather, from their discomfort with the church's success in being what she is called to be. There are people who do not like the church simply because the church, by the nature of its very existence, challenges the shallow, self-centered, adolescent values which many of us have adopted during the past few years. Having spoken of some of the weaknesses of the church, let us now speak of some of her strengths.

Living a religious life would be an easy task were it not for the troublesome presence of other people. The woman who says that she feels more religious when she stays at home on Sunday morning watching Oral Roberts on television, the man who claims to have a more uplifting experience on the golf course than in church, the young person who receives "better vibrations" in twenty minutes of Transcendental Meditation than in sixty minutes of morning worship are all simply stating what is true: It *is* easier to feel "religious" in such individual, solitary, comfortable circumstances. Whether it is possible to be *Christian* in such circumstances is another matter!

John Wesley said that there is no such thing as a "solitary Christian." The faith must be shared in order to be kept. Christianity is a social religion. It becomes dwarfed and blighted when alone; it thrives in numbers. But true to our ruggedly individualistic self-centeredness, we have tried to practice the Christian faith as if it were a home correspondence course in self-improvement. The great heresy in American popular religion is the notion that "religion is a private affair," a secret contract between the believer and God. This individualistic heresy manifests itself in a number of ways.

First, there is the "Me and Jesus" arrangement. Devotees of this cult often tell us there is a difference between "Christianity" and "churchianity," (ignoring all that biblical talk about the church as the "body of Christ" and the question of "How can you love God whom you have not seen if you do not love your neighbor whom you have seen?"). Here, Jesus is transformed into a close, personal friend who listens, comforts, sustains, confirms, agrees, and almost never offends, prods, criticizes, or judges. In this cozy closet religion, Jesus starts to look less like the challenging, demanding Lord of the Bible and more like my own attitudes, prejudices, and values. The ethical demands of Jesus; the command to love our neighbors not only in vague feelings but also in words and deeds; and the commission to be in the world healing, witnessing, and exorcising are forgotten in our preoccupation with Jesus, the "Good Friend" who is there to do things for us as individuals. "What a friend we have in Jesus," the old gospel song proclaims. Jesus is a friend, the friend whom most of us need—the friend who challenges us; pushes us; calls us into life, into the needs of others, and out of ourselves. If we really "take Jesus into our hearts," he will take us out of our selfish concerns and into the swirling mass of suffering humanity. The church challenges the "Me and Jesus" cult by reminding us that true Christianity is an ethical, selfless, outward, neighborly faith.

A recent version (another surrogate of Christianity) of the "Me and Jesus" heresy is what we might call the cult of "Do Your Own Thing." This is the old laissez-faire, rugged individualism redone in a modern idiom. By "Do Your Own Thing," I mean those new surrogates for religious beliefs and practices—the pop psychologies of the human potential movement with its rhetoric of personal growth and self-fulfillment. Building on Freud, the devotees of "est," Transactional Analysis (TA), sensitivity and encounter groups, Gestalt, etc., tell people to become "free" and "liberated" through various techniques for "fulfillment of individual human potential." This usually involves the unblocking of suppressed feelings and the baring of one's inner depths to a group of persons who are engaged in the same undertaking. While the human potential movement has undoubtedly aided many people in living richer lives, it is not without its flaws, and it is a far cry from the discipleship and service which the Christian faith demands.

Like the "Me and Jesus" cult, the new "Do Your Own Thing" techniques urge subjectivistic disengagement from all systems of belief and values in order to find "reality" which is enclosed wholly within one's unconscious life. "Reality" is said to be the end result of the "inward journey" in which you lose touch with the outside in order to get in touch with the inside. Feelings are usually considered more important than beliefs or ideas. At least the "Me and Jesus" cult has the advantage of focusing on Jesus who is a historical person. In "Do Your Own Thing," one finds the truth only as one looks more deeply into one's self. Freud's warnings about "narcissistic regression" are curiously overlooked by the human potential movement. "Est" tells its pilgrims, "You are responsible only for yourself. You are the only one who can give your life meaning." Rules, responsibilities to others, life's moral and emotional ambiguities, and tensions between our potential and our limits are all overlooked. The goal of "Do Your Own Thing" is a romantic return to some inner state of blissful innocence in which (to use TA terminology) our "natural child" is freed from stifling rules and prescriptions of a confining adult world. Here is the old Rousseau myth of natural innocence redone in modern, psychological terms. Here we border on the subjectivistic antinomianism (lawlessness) for which Israel was condemned when everyone did "what was right in his own eyes" (Judges 21:25).

Against these new pop psychologies, the church, by its very existence, affirms that reality is a corporate product, not an individual discovery or the result of following the right technique. The more deeply we look within ourselves, the more we tend to disengage from the truth of history, the demands of our neighbors, and the workings of God in the world. We fragment our subjective selves from the objective world. Subjectivistic truths are the most comfortable truths because they are the ones that we create! I agree with Saint Teresa who said of spiritual introspection, "It is a great grace of God to practice self-examination, but too much is as bad as too little . . . we shall accomplish more by contemplating the Divinity than by keeping our eyes fixed on ourselves." We will "find ourselves" only as we are found by that Other who is the source of our true selfhood. The *real* truth is the truth which comes to us from other people, from the world, and from God. It is truth which sometimes hurts but always frees—freeing us from our excessive self-concern. The church exists to confront people with that brand of uncomfortable truth.

Finally, a third surrogate for the Christian faith which challenges the church today is what my teacher at Yale, Bill Muehl, used to call "Lone Ranger Christianity." You remember the Lone Ranger. He was that anonymous masked marvel on a white horse who traveled throughout the West, aided only by his taciturn friend Tonto and his stallion Silver. The Lone Ranger worked alone, outside the confines of established law and order, without asking the aid of local law enforcement authorities who were usually portrayed in the Lone Ranger vignettes as bumbling incompetents. The Lone Ranger swept down out of nowhere, aiding the innocent and the oppressed, righting wrong, defeating evil, then disappearing in a cloud of dust with a hearty "Hi-Ho, Silver," leaving the recipient of his good works asking the inevitable "Who was that masked man?"

The Lone Ranger motif is still around. How many times have pastors heard the familiar refrain, "Well, I consider myself to be a Christian. I do a lot of good in my own quiet way. I just don't do my good from within the church. I think I can be as good a Christian on my own"? The image of an anonymous do-gooder, quietly going about helping others, is an appealing image; but, alas, it is an image which is more often fantasy than fact. Anonymous do-gooders are hard to find these days mainly because most of the good which needs doing requires corporate, public acts of goodness. To be a true good Samaritan requires risk, long-term involvement, and cost. The safety of anonymity, the ease of impulsive and momentary acts of charity, the impersonality of the detached contribution are behind the real appeal of Lone Ranger beneficence. Most decent people will gladly give a few dollars to help a needy person provide food for his or her children, but we grumble over "government giveaways" and the "welfare mess" which are a relatively inexpensive (when compared with the other things we taxpayers are asked to spend our money on) attempt to arrive at a more long-term, shared, corporate commitment to people in need. We are happy to help poor minority groups as long as they stay in their neighborhoods, their churches, their schools, and as long as we are not forced to come face-to-face with their demands for true equality and dignity.

The Lone Ranger masks himself not necessarily out of humility but, rather, out of a basic egotism which denies that we need other people in order to perform true acts of love. The Lone Ranger works alone because it's safer that way. By his working alone, no one questions the motives, the means, or the results of his "good works." He can live in his simplistic world where good guys wear white hats and bad guys wear black hats. He can do his good, disappear in a cloud of dust, and take no responsibility for the lasting consequences of his actions. The historical record of vigilantes is not good. Vigilantism is illegal because people "take the law into their own hands," interpreting what is right by individualistic codes of conduct and perverting justice in their self-appointed attempt to administer justice.

Justice is a corporate endeavor. It is a rather simple act to leave a basket of food on a poor person's doorstep at Christmastime. It would be a more complicated but infinitely more loving act to work to change the laws, economic systems, and social structures of a society which engenders poverty in the first place. Jesus did say not to let your left hand know what your right hand is doing when you perform an act of love. But this was not a prescription against joining hands with other people to perform more difficult and more lasting acts of love. The church challenges the Lone Rangers and their claim of individualistic, egocentric acts of charity. The church is unpopular with many people because it makes demands upon them. T. S. Eliot once wrote:

Why should men love the Church? Why should they love her laws? She tells them of Life and Death, and of all that they would forget. She is tender where they would be hard, and hard where they like to be soft. She tells them of Evil and Sin, and other unpleasant facts.[1]

That is the very reason that most people dislike the church.

The church asks people to grow. It assumes that Christians are made, not born. It affirms, unlike many of the pop psychologies and methods for personal growth, that human growth is a long, difficult journey which doesn't take place in a weekend. It takes a lifetime. The old revivalists and the new human potentialists seek shortcuts to growth which rarely produce lasting results. The church challenges the widespread notion that what we do naturally is the best that we could do. Given enough Sundays, the church will probably challenge our basic selfishness, our little lies and deceits, our cherished prejudices, and our childish misconceptions. Far from their being in "the comfortable pew," I suspect that most church members are more likely to confront the "unpleasant things" of life inside the church than will their fellow men and women who are outside the church. Growth is often painful. If you can't bear the kind of pain which comes when you have your beloved idols kicked over, when you have your false gods exposed, when you have your falsehoods held up to the harsh light of truth, then you are wise to avoid the church.

The church demands things of people. It challenges the popular notion that "you can't fight city hall," that we human beings are helpless and powerless sheep who have nothing to do with our common destiny. The church will tell you every time it asks you to offer yourself and your gifts, to sing and pray, to listen and act that you have responsibility. In spite of all our efforts to evade responsibility for our world and other people, whether those evasions take the form of "Me and Jesus," "Do Your Own Thing," or the "Lone Ranger," the church lifts up our oneness with humanity under the love of one God. In Jean Paul Sartre's play *No Exit*, three selfish people are trapped for eternity in a room with no doors. "Hell is other people," one character screams in desperation. Hell *is* other people when there is no way to escape our responsibility for them!

Stay in the church long enough, and there is a good chance that it will demand your time, your money, your love, maybe even your life. And it will make no apologies for its nagging demands. The church wants not just our platonic and vague "love" or our abstract "faith"; it wants us to put our money where our hearts are. (Remember what Jesus said about hearts and treasures?) It wants commitment and response. The church will ask you to feel some of the world's aches and pains along with your own. It will challenge your cynicism and defeatism with talk about Easter and "all things being possible." It will tell you that you are more competent and capable, more responsible for yourself and others than you may think you are. The church demands a response from you simply because every time the church opens the Bible, sings a hymn, hears a sermon, baptizes a person, eats the Lord's Supper or a family night potluck supper, the church hears God demanding a response.

The person who says that he or she dislikes the church because it is full of sinners and hypocrites makes the erroneous assumption that we in the church are embarrassed by our clientele. We are not any more embarrassed over our collection of sinners than a hospital is ashamed of its sick people. Sinners, hypocrites, men of little faith, outcasts, the sick, and hurting people were the ones who clustered around Jesus. This rather seedy cast of characters made Jesus not the least bit uncomfortable. They were precisely the reason why Jesus was in the world. Besides, as someone has suggested, today's hypocrites may not be like that self-righteous Pharisee who paraded into the temple while the humble publican stayed outside and prayed, "Lord, have mercy on me a sinner." The new hypocrites may be those outside the church who pray, "God, I thank thee that I am not like all those sinful and hypocritical people in the church."

To be a part of the church is not to suffer from delusions of sainthood (I have met few people in the church with that alleged

fantasy); rather, it is to admit bravely that one has needs, that
one has weaknesses, and that one wishes to work these things out
in the presence of a gracious God and fellow sinners. The main
difference between the sinners inside the church and those on
the outside is that the ones on the inside are free to admit to
some of their sinfulness because they have received some of the
freedom of forgiveness. That is a rather significant difference.

The church is, above all, a group of people, a more human
than a divine institution—that is its glory. It was no accident
that Jesus called a group of disciples, not isolated individuals.
Nor was it by chance that immediately following the death and
resurrection of Jesus we find a group of people gathered together
in the name of Jesus. The Christian life is not an easy one, the
world being what it is and we being what we are. We need others.
Strong people are those who are strong enough to admit that
they need other people. The rugged individualist is a spiritual
adolescent. Such a one deludes oneself into thinking that one
can go it alone. When freedom is defined as "doing your own
thing" or "free to be yourself," it is false freedom which leads to
the enslavement of loneliness and isolation. To be free and strong
enough to respond to other people, to let other people lean on
you, and to learn from other people is to be free indeed.

The basic issue here is not so much what you think about
people or even what you think about the church. The heart of
the matter is what you believe about God. Against all those who
contend that God is to be found by getting inside of oneself or
getting outside of the world, the Christian faith bases itself on the
scandalous belief that God became a man and lived in this world.
The traditional Christian belief in the virgin birth of Jesus is not a
proof that Jesus was divine and extraordinary. It is an affirmation
that, in the birth of Jesus, God entered into the human and the
ordinary. If a common, everyday, simple person like Mary can be
used by God to give the world its salvation, perhaps the rest of us
common, everyday, simple people can be useful, too.

The theological doctrine of the incarnation ("in the body")
says that just as God is revealed in the life, death, and resurrection

of a first-century man named Jesus, so God can be revealed in other men and women today. You cannot find the God of Abraham, Isaac, and Jacob—or for that matter the God of Mary, Peter, and Paul—by withdrawing into your subjectivity or fleeing from the world. You can't because God has chosen to be in the world in the midst of people. The church is an expression of our firm belief in the incarnation. If you don't expect to find God in that fat usher who greets you at the front door on Sunday morning, in the reading of an ancient and disordered book called the Bible, in the quivering solo of that aging soprano who sings in the choir, in the sermons of that well-meaning but poorly endowed preacher, in the smile of that kindly old man or the squirms of the restless toddlers who sit on either side of you on the pew, then there is no point in bothering with the church.

The scandal of the Christian faith, the real stumbling block, is that it points to a Jew from Nazareth ("Can anything good come out of Nazareth?") and says, "This is what the Son of God looks like." The scandal of the church is that it points to a rag-tag conglomeration of partly weak and partly strong, sometimes faithful and sometimes foolish people and says, "This is, what the kingdom of God looks like." The Word has become flesh and dwelt among us. Where two or three are gathered, there God is present. When someone asked Jesus what heaven looked like, he told them that delightful parable of the great banquet in which, when all the nice and proper people turned down the master's invitation, the master then invited all the ragamuffins and rogues, prostitutes and tax collectors to eat at his table. If you can't believe that the kingdom of heaven looks like that banquet table, then you'll never believe that the church looks like that struggling group of sinners over at old First Church who eat around the Communion table.

When I was serving in my first student pastorate in Georgia, I remember complaining to a seminary professor about how disappointed I had been over the poor quality of my church members. They had shocked me with their marital problems, their lack of commitment, and their general backwardness.

Frankly, I thought that I deserved better. After listening to my long complaint, the professor replied, "But the shocking thing is that Jesus said that people like them would be entering the kingdom first. What do you do with that?"

I look at the church today and am scandalized by our unfaithfulness, our lethargy, our timidity. I see betrayal, ignorance, fear, self-centeredness, complacency, and pride within our ranks. In short, I see modern disciples who distinctly resemble the scandalousness of those first twelve disciples. The Gospel writers go to great lengths to demonstrate that these first disciples were anything but saints. And yet, it was to these people that Jesus left the keys to the kingdom. He left them in charge of his work and his holdings until he got back. It was to these people that he revealed the secret that many of the people who look strong in this world are really weak and many of the people who look weak are really strong (and he was referring to people like them). To these people, gathered together simply because they all had the same Master and knew that they all needed one another to be truly about their Master's business, to these people he gave the power to turn the kingdoms of this world upside down even as the world thought that it had put an end to all this talk about a kingdom of God.

One of the charges which the Pharisees leveled against Jesus was that he ate and drank with sinners. Every time the church eats and drinks the Lord's Supper, it is claiming that Jesus chooses the same kind of dinner companions today!

For Adults Only

I n a delightful essay, "The Shadow of Great-Grandmama's Dress," in her book *Yes, World*, Mary Jean Irion notes that "in matters of deepest importance the church does not proceed on the faith of our fathers, but on the faith of the little old ladies."[1] How many times have we seen a church attempt to confront boldly the problems of faith in our turbulent world, to revitalize its worship, to make religion relevant to people, and then someone utters those seven deadly words, *"What would the little old ladies think?"* And zap, that's the end of that!

In our concern not to irritate Great-grandmama, we have so tamed and restricted the faith that Christianity has all the bite and boldness of an angel food cake with marshmallow icing. If the people in the pew know anything about theology's recent struggles, about new advances in biblical scholarship, they have likely learned it on their own. They will rarely hear it from the pulpit ever since Pastor X and Pastor Y reassured themselves, "You can't say things like that to the little old ladies—it would destroy their faith."

That "faith" which we so diligently protect is most often a set of childish misconceptions, anachronistic beliefs, and simplistic attitudes which would collapse in the face of serious examination. If they were examined from the pulpit or church school classroom, Great-grandmama might have to face up to reality and do some growing, and that, we assume, Great-grandmama could never do. And that which cannot be told to Great-grandmama is not told to anybody. The words and deeds of the church are carefully weighed and filtered until they become the soggy milk toast which doesn't faintly resemble the gospel.

If this is a fair estimate of what happens in many of our churches, it is unfair to single out one particular age and gender as representative of this type of closed, naive, immature Christianity. This mindset is by no means limited to little old ladies. I have met strapping teenagers, overweight clergypersons, college women, and tall middle-aged businessmen who are of the same intellectual stripe. Their bodies may be young and vibrant, but their minds and spirits are hardened and old. They have that "simple faith" which is often a nice way of saying that they refuse to risk themselves and are determined never to think or to grow.

It is regrettable that little old ladies have been singled out as the stereotype of this flaccid version of Christianity. I had not been a minister long before I discovered those bright-eyed, white-haired girls who destroy the "little-old-lady" image with their "You tell 'em, son," when I had said more than I should have said, or their slightly risqué joke about some event from the good old days. I found that most of my older church members, perhaps because they had lived longer than the rest of us or had experienced more of life's vicissitudes or had discovered over the years how difficult discipleship can be, were more persistent than younger people in calling the church to speak to all of faith's demands.

No, Great-grandmama comes in all shapes, genders, and ages. She is anyone who would rather remain in the world as it was rather than venture forth into the world as it could be, who would cling to infantile gods and childish hopes rather than grow. The teenager looking for a set of neat, easy solutions to every problem in life, the middle-aged couple wanting the church to condone their shallow values and cherished prejudices, the older person wanting a six-year-old church school faith to carry him through his sixties are the real "little old ladies."

And what brutal beast would be so cruel as to tamper with the beliefs of the little old ladies? Why not just accept their fragile faith; tell them, "It doesn't matter what you believe as long as you're sincere"; and continue to protect, insulate, and ensure Great-grandmother from having to come face to face with the fullness of the Christian faith? I'll tell you why we must not leave the great-grandmothers (of any age or gender) alone—because life is tough and demanding. There are people in the world who see little old ladies only as things to be used, abused, and taken advantage of. When a person comes up against doubt or tragedy, when a person comes face to face with the complexities of life, he or she will not appreciate that the church protected his or her mind in more tranquil times. In our overprotective, hothouse environment, we have produced weak Christians. Christianity means much more than simply being nice to people, even to nice people like Great-grandmama.

Jesus was not "nice" to people. He knew, from personal experience, that life is no afternoon tea party. What right do we have to protect anyone from achieving his or her full spiritual maturity and strength? Most people, inside or outside the church, are not as simpleminded and weak, not as defenseless and fragile as we often assume they are. Sometimes we ministers excuse our own spiritual sluggishness by blaming our timidity on our concern for the faith of Great-grandmama.

What about the little old ladies? Well, what about the teenagers facing a permissive and valueless society; or the young couple on the verge of a divorce; or the beleaguered businessperson; the despairing welfare mother; the bored and trapped housewife; the lonely senior citizen; or the person who has given up on the Christian faith, having decided that it is only a crutch for unthinking weaklings? What about *them?*

Back in the Book of Genesis, when old Abraham and Sarah were getting on in years (Abraham was a hundred at the time; Sarah was ninety), God had some fun with them. God told Abraham that Sarah was finally going to have a baby. Abraham, thinking it was all a kind of cruel joke, "fell on his face and laughed," as Genesis tells it (17:17). In another version of the story, Sarah, despite her denials when God asked her about it, had a good laugh herself. But the joke was on them. Nine months later, the old woman gave birth to her first son, calling him "Isaac," which means "laughter" in Hebrew. She laughed all the way from the geriatric ward to the maternity ward.

Sarah and Abraham laughed because this was an outrageous thing to do to a woman of ninety. Frederick Buechner says they laughed at the thought of the divine having such a crazy sense of humor.[2] They laughed because, if it all turned out to be true, they would really have something to smile about. They laughed because, even at their advanced age, they still had some growing to do. I think the moral of this story is that God likes to surprise little old ladies. God believes in us and our capabilities much more than we believe in ourselves. We are not as weak, limited, and finished as we think we are.

God has surprises in store for all of us little old ladies of every age and gender.

As with Abraham and Sarah, God calls us to venture forth into some strange places. Abraham left the cozy land of his forefathers and journeyed into an unknown land simply because he felt that God was leading him forward. It was tempting to stay behind in more familiar terrain, but Abraham knew that our God is a living, moving God who lets us stop just long enough to catch our breath and then beckons us on. As the angel said to the women who went out to the tomb on Easter morning expecting to find the dead body of Jesus, "He is not here—he is going on before you!"

Abraham and Sarah ventured out by faith, which is to say that they traveled on trust. They trusted God because they felt that God trusted them. Childless, at a seemingly impotent old age, Abraham believed the crazy promise that he would father a nation. He believed because God seemed to believe in him. They were like Mary who called herself the "handmaid of the Lord," which means that she told the angel Gabriel to tell God, "I don't know what you're going to ask me to do, but I'll do it anyway." Or as Mary's Son said in similarly uncertain circumstances, "Not my will but thine be done." It can be the same for us. We are not as weak, as helpless, as evil as we sometimes think we are. We have strengths and abilities which we have not even discovered. All we need is to be open to a few surprises, a few laughs when the joke is on us, a few journeys into some unknown territory. Christianity is only for adults—spiritual adults of any age. Substitutes for faith promise us security, salvation, peace, and joy without any risk or trust on our part. Substitutes will tell us to be content with where we are rather than explore where we could be. They are all false faiths, for they require no faith, no trust, no risk, no growth.

True faith, the kind to which Jesus calls us, is "the assurance of things hoped for, the conviction of things not seen" (Hebrews 11:1). It is a process, not a possession. It gives us something to chew on for the rest of our lives. Faith is certitude in the midst of doubt rather than certainty with no doubts. Faith is a journey with a compass which points us in the right direction, not a detailed map which tells us every step to take. Faith is not being sure of where you are going but going anyway because you like the traveling companions and you know who leads the way. Faith is a journey which you do not wait to begin until you are desperate and have nowhere else to go or until you are devastated and miserable and are forced to go; faith is going because you have heard the good news that the Guide is trustworthy and that the trip is worth the cost.

The first Christians were called "followers of the Way."

I close by showing you a picture which means much to me. It was painted by the fifteenth-century Italian painter Piero della Francesca, on a wall of the town hall in a little Italian village. It is called *The Resurrection.* The scene is Easter morning, just at dawn. Piero gives us a vision of Christ rising from the tomb. At the base of the tomb sleep four Roman soldiers, resting on their spears and shields. Here are Caesar's men with Caesar's symbols who have been sent to guard the tomb. They sleep, blind to the miracle which is taking place in their midst. They assume that Caesar and his legions had the last word in the Jesus episode. They are wrong.

Above them, Christ rises out of the cold tomb, rising from death to life. The wounds of his crucifixion are visible in his side, hands, and feet. The wounds are bloody reminders of the deeds of an evil world which treats its saviors and its criminals in the same way. His foot is placed firmly on the side of the tomb. The cross, a symbol of shame, suffering, and humiliation, has been transformed into an insignia of victory. Christ now bears it like a triumphant battle flag. The powers and principalities of evil have been met and defeated. Christ's body is incarnate, visible, fleshly proof of that victory. In

The Resurrection—Piero della Francesca

the left background, the landscape is in the grip of winter and desolation. There are no leaves on the trees, no signs of life. On the right, the rooftops of a village can be seen, and the trees show the first green leaves of spring. Not only has Christ moved from death to life but, through his work, the world has moved and is moving from death to life, from winter to spring as well. The first light of dawn signifies that some great cosmic transformation is beginning. The whole world is being made new.

I remember the first time I saw this painting. I was in college, spending a summer with some friends traveling around Europe. I had driven over a hot, dusty, bumpy road through the Italian countryside. As the road wound interminably through one little village after another and the day dragged on, I began to wonder if the journey was worth it. When I entered the Palazzo Comunale at Borgo San Sepolcro, looked down the hall, and gazed upon. *The Resurrection* covering the rear wall, I knew the trip had been worth it.

The Resurrection sticks in my mind even today as a strong, bold, penetrating vision of Christ as our Good News, the best news we have received in two thousand years. We need to recover that vision of strength today, the strength which first delivers us from all which would devastate us and which then gives us a place in the continuing deliverance of our world. Amen!

Notes

Chapter 2

1   Colin Morris, *The Word and the Words* (Nashville: Abingdon Press, 1975), 21.

Chapter 3

1   Dana Prom Smith, *The Debonaire Disciple* (Philadelphia: Fortress Press, 1973), 3.

2   Paul Tillich, *The New Being* (New York: Charles Scribner's Sons, 1955), 7, 9.

Chapter 4

1   William Shakespeare, *The Merchant of Venice*, act 1, sc. 3, line 97.

2   Oral Roberts, *The Miracle of Seed-Faith* (Tulsa, OK: Oral Roberts Evangelistic Association, 1970), 21.

3   Roberts, *The Miracle of Seed-Faith*, 118.

Chapter 5

1   Dietrich Bonhoeffer, *Letters and Papers from Prison*, ed. Eberhard Bethge (New York: Macmillan, 1953), 209.

2   Bonhoeffer, *Letters and Papers from Prison*, 214.

3   Bonhoeffer, *Letters and Papers from Prison*, 209–10.

4   Bonhoeffer, *Letters and Papers from Prison*, 13–14.

Chapter 6

1   "Eucharistic Prayer of Hippolytus" in Lucien Deiss, *Early Sources of the Liturgy* (Staten Island, NY: Alba House, 1967), alt., 38–41.

2   W. H. Auden, *The Collected Poetry of W. H. Auden* (New York: Random House, Inc., 1945), 457.

3   Paul Tillich, *The Eternal Now* (New York: Charles Scribner's Sons, 1963), 179.

4   John Killinger, ed., *The Eleven O'clock News and Other Experimental Sermons* (Nashville: Abingdon Press, 1975), 30.

Chapter 7

1   Harry Emerson Fosdick, *The Living of These Days* (New York: Harper & Row, Publishers, 1956), 242.

2   Smith, *The Debonaire Disciple*, 68.

3   Eric Fromm, *The Art of Loving* (New York: Harper & Row, 1956), 22–23.

Chapter 8

1   T. S. Eliot, "Choruses from 'The Rock,'" in *The Complete Poems and Plays, 1909-1950* (New York: Harcourt Brace Jovanovich, 1952), 106.

Chapter 9

1   Mary Jean Irion, *Yes, World* (New York: Cambria Press, 1970), 92.

2   Frederick Buechner, *Wishful Thinking: A Theological ABC* (New York: Harper & Row, 1973), 25.

About Paraclete Press

Who We Are

As the publishing arm of the Community of Jesus, Paraclete Press presents a full expression of Christian belief and practice—from Catholic to Evangelical, from Protestant to Orthodox, reflecting the ecumenical charism of the Community and its dedication to sacred music, the fine arts, and the written word. We publish books, recordings, sheet music, and video/DVDs that nourish the vibrant life of the church and its people.

What We Are Doing

BOOKS | PARACLETE PRESS BOOKS show the richness and depth of what it means to be Christian. While Benedictine spirituality is at the heart of who we are and all that we do, our books reflect the Christian experience across many cultures, time periods, and houses of worship.

We have many series, including *Paraclete Essentials; Paraclete Fiction; Paraclete Poetry; Paraclete Giants;* and for children and adults, *All God's Creatures,* books about animals and faith; and *San Damiano Books,* focusing on Franciscan spirituality. Others include *Voices from the Monastery* (men and women monastics writing about living a spiritual life today), *Active Prayer,* and new for young readers: *The Pope's Cat.* We also specialize in gift books for children on the occasions of Baptism and First Communion, as well as other important times in a child's life, and books that bring creativity and liveliness to any adult spiritual life.

The MOUNT TABOR BOOKS series focuses on the arts and literature as well as liturgical worship and spirituality; it was created in conjunction with the Mount Tabor Ecumenical Centre for Art and Spirituality in Barga, Italy.

MUSIC | The PARACLETE RECORDINGS label represents the internationally acclaimed choir *Gloriæ Dei Cantores,* the *Gloriæ Dei Cantores Schola,* and the other instrumental artists of the *Arts Empowering Life Foundation.*

Paraclete Press is the exclusive North American distributor for the Gregorian chant recordings from St. Peter's Abbey in Solesmes, France. Paraclete also carries all of the Solesmes chant publications for Mass and the Divine Office, as well as their academic research publications.

In addition, PARACLETE PRESS SHEET MUSIC publishes the work of today's finest composers of sacred choral music, annually reviewing over 1,000 works and releasing between 40 and 60 works for both choir and organ.

VIDEO | Our video/DVDs offer spiritual help, healing, and biblical guidance for a broad range of life issues including grief and loss, marriage, forgiveness, facing death, understanding suicide, bullying, addictions, Alzheimer's, and Christian formation.

Learn more about us at our website:

www.paracletepress.com

or phone us toll-free at 1.800.451.5006

SCAN
TO
READ